Conquer New Standards

Literary Text

Table of Contents

Introduction 4

Letters to Parents/Guardians 12

Unit 1: Answer Questions Using Details 14
"Freddy Won't Speak" • Poem

Unit 2: Ask and Answer Questions Using Details 18
"Bed in Summer" • Poem

Unit 3: Recount the Story 22
"Consider the Shoe" • Fairy Tale

Unit 4: Identify Central Message 26
"The Talking Eggs" • Folktale

Unit 5: Describe Characters 30
"Little Tío" • Realistic Fiction

Unit 6: How Characters' Actions Contribute to Plot 34
"How Anansi Got Long, Thin Legs" • Myth

Unit 7: Meaning of Words and Phrases 38
"Octavia and the Numbers" • Realistic Fiction

Unit 8: Literal and Nonliteral Language 42
"Gray Makes a Move" • Realistic Fiction

Unit 9: Parts of Texts 46
Excerpt from "Little White Lily" • Poem

Unit 10: How Texts Build 50
"The New Menu" • Realistic Fiction

Unit 11: Point of View of Characters 54
"Walking With Ruby" • Historical Fiction

Unit 12: Point of View of Narrator 58
"Race Day" • Fantasy

Unit 13: Describe Mood Using Illustrations and Text 62
"Fire the Goat and Flim the Goose," an excerpt from *Sand Flat Shadows* • Fantasy

Unit 14: Describe Characters Using Illustrations and Text . . .66
Excerpt from "Pittypat and Tippytoe" • Poem

Unit 15: Describe Setting Using Illustrations and Text 70
"A Mysterious Matter" • Mystery

Unit 16: Compare/Contrast Themes of Two Texts 74
"Zula Speaks" • Mystery
"Sadie Signs" • Adventure Story

Unit 17: Compare/Contrast Settings of Two Texts 80
Excerpt from "The Old Lobsterman" • Poem
Excerpt from "Menotomy Lake (Spy Pond)" • Poem

Unit 18: Compare/Contrast Plots of Two Texts. 86
Adapted excerpt from "Honor Bright, President" • Fiction
Adapted excerpt from "The Going-To Club" • Fiction

Discussion Prompts & At-Home Activities. 92
Answer Key 110

Introduction

Many states have adopted standards that set clear expectations about what students need to learn at each grade level. The standards are designed to be rigorous and pertinent to the real world, and they reflect the knowledge and skills that our young people need for success in college and careers.

Why *Conquer New Standards: Literary Text*?
As a teacher, you are required to incorporate these standards into your lesson plans. Your students may need targeted practice in order to meet grade-level standards and be promoted to the next grade.

Conquer New Standards: Literary Text provides you with ready-to-go units that support students in the development of key skills outlined in the standards (see the chart on page 5). Each unit includes one or more passages as well as a model of a response to a question about that passage. After reading the passage and reviewing the model, students practice applying the modeled skill by answering a variety of questions, including constructed response and multiple choice.

> **This book is appropriate for on-grade-level students as well as for English Learners and those requiring intervention.**

Many state standards have these key expectations:	In *Conquer New Standards: Literary Text*, students will:	
Students must read a "staircase" of increasingly complex texts in order to be ready for the demands of college and career-level reading.	• Read passages independently. • Encounter a range of complex passages.	
Students must read a diverse array of classic and contemporary literature from around the world. Students must come to understand other perspectives and cultures.	• Read classic literature. • Read contemporary literature. • Read about a wide diversity of characters and cultures as well as stories from around the world. • Read a variety of genres: fiction, poetry, drama, myths, and more.	
Students must show a "steadily growing ability" to comprehend and analyze text.	• Engage in a focused review of specific text comprehension skills. • Develop their understanding of each skill through modeled examples. • Encounter assessment items in each unit that test the unit skill as well as skills reviewed earlier in the book.	
Students must respond critically to three main text types: opinion/ argument, informational, and narrative.	• Read a variety of narrative texts and have multiple opportunities to develop responses.	The companion book, *Conquer New Standards: Informational Text,* offers students opportunities to respond to opinion/ argument and informational texts.
Students must engage effectively in a range of collaborative discussions (one-on-one, in groups, and teacher-led) with diverse partners on appropriate topics and texts, building on others' ideas and expressing their own clearly.	• Discuss skills and engage in skill-focused activities with teachers, peers, and parents/guardians to extend their understanding of skills.	
Students explain how a text's illustrations contribute to the meaning of a literary text.	• Encounter texts involving illustrations and pictures.	
Students must value evidence.	• Answer a wide array of assessment questions, both multiple-choice and open-ended, using evidence gathered from supplied passages to support their responses.	

What You'll Find in This Book

This book offers skill-specific units with appealing texts and assessment-style questions, discussion prompts to further student understanding, and activities—all of which can be used in the classroom for independent work or as homework assignments. When used as homework, the units are a great way to foster a home-school connection. The materials in this book are also great for small- and whole-group lessons. See page 11 for suggestions about how to use the units in a variety of settings.

The Units

Each unit begins with either a single text or a pair of texts.

Before assigning the first unit for students to do independently, model how to read—and reread—a passage.

1. Think about the purpose for reading the passage.

2. Read the passage all the way through to get the gist of it.

3. Reread the passage again, more slowly.

4. Refer to the passage to answer the questions.

Target Skill
Each unit includes a target skill that students will review and practice throughout the unit.

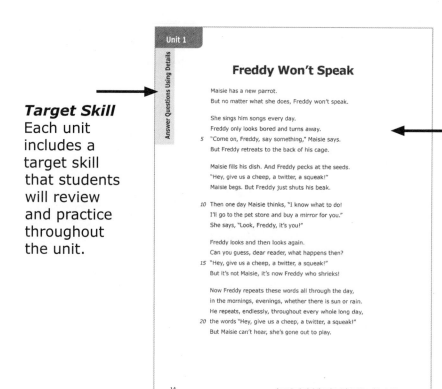

On-Level Texts
All of the texts have been created to offer grade-appropriate reading experiences for students. Students should read the passages independently. Avoid front-loading information or pre-teaching vocabulary. This will provide students with practice similar to the assessments they will eventually take.

Modeling and Tips

Each unit provides a page with a brief review of the skill along with a sample question, an explanation of the sample answer, and an additional opportunity for students to apply their learning at home.

Review the Skill

This section provides a focused description of the unit's skill as a helpful reminder to students.

Home-School Connection

A Home-School Connection activity is provided in each unit. It provides a brief activity allowing parents and guardians to build on what students are learning in school. The activity is focused on the unit skill and involves everyday materials.

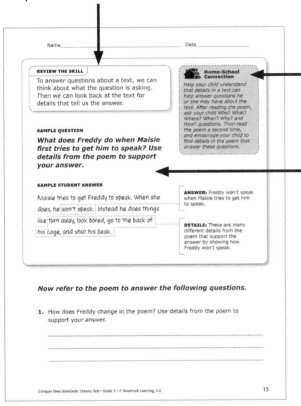

Sample Question and Sample Answer

Each unit offers a sample question focused on the unit skill followed by a sample student answer. Clues guide students to better understand how the sample answer uses text evidence to accurately and comprehensively answer the sample question. This section of each unit models how to read, answer, and provide text support with an assessment-style question, so that students are better prepared to answer questions independently.

Independent Practice

Each unit provides a variety of assessment-style questions. Students will encounter multiple-choice questions with single correct answers, multiple-choice questions with several correct answers, two-part questions, and open-ended questions requiring them to write short, constructed responses. These questions give students opportunities to apply their understanding of the unit skill and show their comprehension of the unit text. Students can work through these items independently to become experienced assessment takers.

Multiple-Choice Questions

Two-Part Questions

Constructed-Response Question

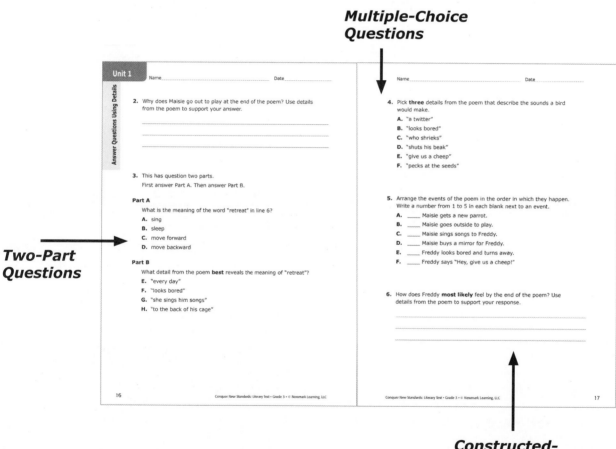

Conquer New Standards: Literary Text • Grade 3 • © Newmark Learning, LLC

Discuss and Share

At the back of the book, you will find additional resources to support students in becoming successful readers. Sentence starters are provided for each unit to make it easy to encourage further discussion of unit texts and skills. Additional at-home activities can be used to help students and their families build greater real-world connections and a deeper understanding of the reading skills.

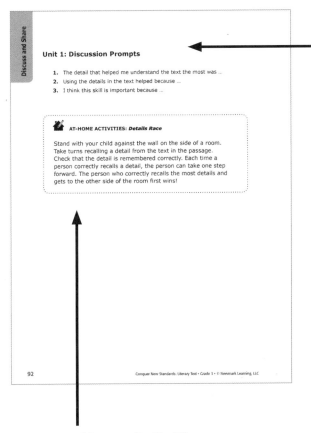

Discussion Prompts
Encourage students to talk about the skills they just reviewed. Through discussion, students can identify areas of confusion, build on each other's thoughts, and phrase skills in their own words. These prompts can be used either in the classroom, in small-group and whole-group settings, or at home to encourage a deeper consideration of important reading comprehension skills.

At-Home Activities
For each unit, there is a quick activity focused on the skill. These activities provide kinesthetic, auditory, visual, and cooperative learning experiences.

Answer Key

Each book contains an answer key that includes rationales and sample answers. Teachers may choose to do the following:

- Review students' responses themselves.
- Assign students to review their own responses or work with a partner to review each other's responses.
- Send the answer key home so that parents or guardians can review students' responses.

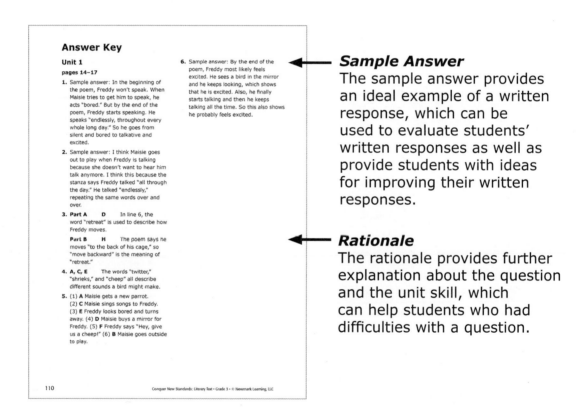

Answer Key

Unit 1

pages 14–17

1. Sample answer: In the beginning of the poem, Freddy won't speak. When Maisie tries to get him to speak, he acts "bored." But by the end of the poem, Freddy starts speaking. He speaks "endlessly, throughout every whole long day." So he goes from silent and bored to talkative and excited.

2. Sample answer: I think Maisie goes out to play when Freddy is talking because she doesn't want to hear him talk anymore. I think this because the stanza says Freddy talked "all through the day." He talked "endlessly," repeating the same words over and over.

3. **Part A**   **D**   In line 6, the word "retreat" is used to describe how Freddy moves.

   Part B   **H**   The poem says he moves "to the back of his cage," so "move backward" is the meaning of "retreat."

4. **A, C, E**   The words "twitter," "shrieks," and "cheep" all describe different sounds a bird might make.

5. (1) **A** Maisie gets a new parrot. (2) **C** Maisie sings songs to Freddy. (3) **E** Freddy looks bored and turns away. (4) **D** Maisie buys a mirror for Freddy. (5) **F** Freddy says "Hey, give us a cheep!" (6) **B** Maisie goes outside to play.

6. Sample answer: By the end of the poem, Freddy most likely feels excited. He sees a bird in the mirror and he keeps looking, which shows that he is excited. Also, he finally starts talking and then he keeps talking all the time. So this also shows he probably feels excited.

110   Conquer New Standards: Literary Text • Grade 3 • © Newmark Learning, LLC

Sample Answer

The sample answer provides an ideal example of a written response, which can be used to evaluate students' written responses as well as provide students with ideas for improving their written responses.

Rationale

The rationale provides further explanation about the question and the unit skill, which can help students who had difficulties with a question.

How to Use *Conquer New Standards: Literary Text*

This book has been designed so that students can work independently—either in class or at home—making it easy for you to reinforce standards mastery without sacrificing valuable teaching time. But the units also work well for small- and whole-group lessons. The chart below outlines some ideas for incorporating the units into your teaching.

If you want to use this book ENTIRELY for classroom work:		
Units	Answer Key	Discuss and Share
Assign students to work on the units independently in class.	Review students' work using the answer key, OR allow students to grade their own work with the answer key.	Use the discussion prompts to lead small-group or whole-group discussions. Use the activities as opportunities for independent, partnered, small-group, or whole-group experiences.

If you want to use this book for a COMBINATION of classroom work and homework:		
Units	Answer Key	Discuss and Share
Assign students to work on the units independently in class.	Review students' work using the answer key, OR allow students to grade their own work with the answer key.	Use the discussion prompts to lead small-group or whole-group discussions.
		Copy the activities and send home as homework opportunities for the student to complete with a parent or guardian.

If you want to use this book ENTIRELY for homework:		
Units	Answer Key	Discuss and Share
Copy the Parent/Guardian Letter and units and send home for students to do as homework.	Copy the answer key for students, parents, or guardian to use to review the students' work.	Copy the discussion prompts and activities to send home as homework, encouraging parent/guardian involvement.

Dear Parent or Guardian,

This year, your child will be completing literary text units for homework. The goal of these units is to ensure that your child has the skills necessary to comprehend a variety of key literary text types, such as stories, poems, folktales and myths, and more.

There are three parts in the take-home unit:
1) the literary text passage
2) a review of the skill being addressed that includes a sample question and sample answer about the text
3) questions about the passage for your child to answer

Encourage your child to read each passage independently if possible, and then review the skill and the sample question and answer. Finally, have him or her answer the unit questions.

The unit also includes engaging activities for you to do with your child at home to further support his or her understanding.

We hope you'll agree that the skills practice that *Conquer New Standards: Literary Text* offers will not only help your child to become a better reader, but also provide him or her with the support needed to become a more successful student.

Estimados padres o tutores:

La tarea de su hija(o) para este año consiste en leer y practicar ejercicios de unidades de textos literarios. El objetivo de estas unidades es garantizar que su hija(o) posea las destrezas necesarias para entender una amplia variedad de textos literarios como poemas, historias, cuentos populares y mitos, y mucho más.

La unidad de la tarea en casa consta de tres partes:
1) el pasaje de texto literario
2) un repaso de la destreza a desarrollar, que incluye ejemplos de pregunta y respuesta sobre el texto
3) preguntas acerca del pasaje para que su hija(o) las responda

Anime a su hija(o) a leer cada pasaje de manera independiente, si es posible. Después, repase la destreza y los ejemplos de pregunta y respuesta. Para terminar, pídale que responda las preguntas de la unidad.

La unidad también incluye entretenidas actividades para que las hagan juntos en casa. Esto apoyará aún más la habilidad de comprensión de su hija(o).

Confiamos en que estará de acuerdo que la práctica de destrezas que ofrece *Conquer New Standards: Literary Text,* ayudará a su hija(o) a ser mejor lector(a) y, además, le brinda el apoyo necesario para ser un(a) estudiante de éxito.

Freddy Won't Speak

Maisie has a new parrot.

But no matter what she does, Freddy won't speak.

She sings him songs every day.

Freddy only looks bored and turns away.

5 "Come on, Freddy, say something," Maisie says.

But Freddy retreats to the back of his cage.

Maisie fills his dish. And Freddy pecks at the seeds.

"Hey, give us a cheep, a twitter, a squeak!"

Maisie begs. But Freddy just shuts his beak.

10 Then one day Maisie thinks, "I know what to do!

I'll go to the pet store and buy a mirror for you."

She says, "Look, Freddy, it's you!"

Freddy looks and then looks again.

Can you guess, dear reader, what happens then?

15 "Hey, give us a cheep, a twitter, a squeak!"

But it's not Maisie, it's now Freddy who shrieks!

Now Freddy repeats these words all through the day,

in the mornings, evenings, whether there is sun or rain.

He repeats, endlessly, throughout every whole long day,

20 the words "Hey, give us a cheep, a twitter, a squeak!"

But Maisie can't hear, she's gone out to play.

REVIEW THE SKILL

To answer questions about a text, we can think about what the question is asking. Then we can look back at the text for details that tell us the answer.

Home-School Connection

Help your child understand that details in a text can help answer questions he or she may have about the text. After reading the poem, ask your child Who? What? Where? When? Why? and How? questions. Then read the poem a second time, and encourage your child to find details in the poem that answer these questions.

SAMPLE QUESTION

What does Freddy do when Maisie first tries to get him to speak? Use details from the poem to support your answer.

SAMPLE STUDENT ANSWER

Maisie tries to get Freddy to speak. When she does, he won't speak. Instead he does things like turn away, look bored, go to the back of his cage, and shut his beak.

ANSWER: Freddy won't speak when Maisie tries to get him to speak.

DETAILS: These are many different details from the poem that support the answer by showing how Freddy won't speak.

Now refer to the poem to answer the following questions.

1. How does Freddy change in the poem? Use details from the poem to support your answer.

_____

_____

_____

2. Why does Maisie go out to play at the end of the poem? Use details from the poem to support your answer.

_____

_____

_____

3. This has question two parts.

First answer Part A. Then answer Part B.

Part A

What is the meaning of the word "retreat" in line 6?

A. sing

B. sleep

C. move forward

D. move backward

Part B

What detail from the poem **best** reveals the meaning of "retreat"?

E. "every day"

F. "looks bored"

G. "she sings him songs"

H. "to the back of his cage"

4. Pick **three** details from the poem that describe the sounds a bird would make.

   A. "a twitter"

   B. "looks bored"

   C. "who shrieks"

   D. "shuts his beak"

   E. "give us a cheep"

   F. "pecks at the seeds"

5. Arrange the events of the poem in the order in which they happen. Write a number from 1 to 6 in each blank next to an event.

   A. _____ Maisie gets a new parrot.

   B. _____ Maisie goes outside to play.

   C. _____ Maisie sings songs to Freddy.

   D. _____ Maisie buys a mirror for Freddy.

   E. _____ Freddy looks bored and turns away.

   F. _____ Freddy says "Hey, give us a cheep!"

6. How does Freddy **most likely** feel by the end of the poem? Use details from the poem to support your response.

   _____

   _____

   _____

Bed in Summer

Robert Louis Stevenson

In winter I get up at night
And dress by yellow candlelight.
In summer, quite the other way,
I have to go to bed by day.

5   I have to go to bed and see
The birds still hopping on the tree,
Or hear the grown-up people's feet
Still going past me in the street.

And does it not seem hard to you,
10 When all the sky is clear and blue,
And I should like so much to play,
To have to go to bed by day?

Asking questions helps us identify when we are confused. Many questions can be answered by going back and looking for details in the text.

SAMPLE QUESTION

In summertime, does the author go to bed when it is dark outside? Use details from the poem in your answer.

SAMPLE STUDENT ANSWER

No, in the summer, the author goes to sleep when it is light out. He says he lights a candle in winter but "in summer, quite the other way." That means in summer, he doesn't need a candle because it's light out. In the next line, he says "I have to go to bed by day."

DETAIL 1: The phrase "in summer, quite the other way" says the author is doing the opposite of what he did in winter.

DETAIL 2: The line "I have to go to bed by day" tells what it's like outside when the author goes to sleep.

Now refer to "Bed in Summer" to answer the questions.

1. Describe two things that happen outside while the author goes to bed. Use details from the poem to support your answer.

_____

_____

_____

Name_____ Date_____

2. Reread this stanza from the poem.

"I have to go to bed and see

The birds still hopping on the tree,

Or hear the grown-up people's feet

Still going past me in the street."

Which words show that the author sleeps by a window?
Choose **two.**

A. "birds"

B. "going"

C. "have"

D. "street"

E. "tree"

3. What is the meaning of the word "candlelight" in line 2?

A. night light

B. light from a lamp

C. light from the sun

D. light from a candle

4. In winter, what does the author do while it's still dark out?

A. play outside

B. get dressed

C. hop on a tree

D. look at the sky

Conquer New Standards: Literary Text • Grade 3 • © Newmark Learning, LLC

5. This question has two parts.

First, answer Part A. Then, answer Part B.

Part A

How does the speaker feel about going to bed at the end of the poem?

A. bored

B. confused

C. happy

D. sad

Part B

Which detail from the poem **best** supports your answer to Part A?

E. "I get up at night."

F. "still going past me"

G. "quite the other way"

H. "I should like so much to play"

6. How does the author think the reader would feel in the same situation? Use details from the poem to support your response.

_____

_____

_____

Consider the Shoe

1   Bippity-boppity … OH PHOO! Doesn't anyone consider me, the Shoe?

2   Yes, me, the Shoe! You remember, from that beloved fairy tale about Cinderella who goes to the ball and meets the prince and blah blah blah …

3   Let me tell you that there is another side to that story. My side!

4   Day by day, Cinderella would sweep and mop and scrub. And her wicked stepmother and stepsisters were cruel to her in return.

5   Then came Cinderella's fairy godmother. With her magic wand, she transformed Cinderella's rags into a beautiful gown. And to complete it all—a pair of magnificent glass slippers! At first, it was exciting to be a part of Cinderella's ensemble. (I looked good with that dress.) But do you think that a wave of a wand could truly clean those work-a-day feet? No! It didn't happen.

6   Then it was time for the ball. Cinderella and the prince danced and danced until midnight. The sweat, oh, the sweat! (Glass slippers don't breathe so well.) I thought I caught a break when she ran off and left me on the stairs. But the prince had to go and find me.

7   He brought me around the kingdom so all the girls could try me on. Oh, the corns and the calluses and the bunions I experienced! Ick. You know how this ends. Yup, once old Stinky Feet tried me on, it was happily ever after. So when anyone "oohs" and "ahs" about Cinderella's story, I, the Shoe, say "PEE-YEW!"

REVIEW THE SKILL

When we recount a story, we remember the most important characters, details, and events.

Home-School Connection

You can help your child practice recounting stories by having him or her tell you a favorite bedtime story. If your child gets stuck trying to remember the story's events, ask questions like "What happened next? How did the character feel about that?"

SAMPLE QUESTION

What was Cinderella's life like at the beginning of the story? Use details from the story in your answer.

SAMPLE STUDENT ANSWER

Cinderella didn't have a very good life. She spent most of her time sweeping, mopping, and scrubbing the floors. Her stepmother and stepsisters were "cruel" to her.

DETAIL 1: These details show what Cinderella did every day.

DETAIL 2: This detail explains how she was treated.

Now refer to "Consider the Shoe" to answer the questions.

1. Describe how the Shoe feels about Cinderella. Use details from the story to support your answer.

_____

_____

_____

Name_____ Date_____

2. When does the Shoe enter Cinderella's story?

  A. The Shoe was a gift from Cinderella's mother before the story began.

  B. The Shoe is given to Cinderella by her fairy godmother.

  C. The Shoe first belongs to one of the wicked stepsisters.

  D. The Shoe is found on the steps of the palace.

3. Look at the cause-and-effect box.

Cause	Effect
	Cinderella's feet get sweaty.

Which detail from the passage goes in the "cause" box?

  A. "He brought me around the kingdom so all the girls could try me on."

  B. "Cinderella and the prince danced and danced until midnight."

  C. "And to complete it all—a pair of magnificent glass slippers!"

  D. "Doesn't anyone consider me, the Shoe?"

4. Arrange the events from the passage in the order in which they happen. Write a number from 1 to 6 in each blank next to an event.

  A. _____ The prince finds the Shoe.

  B. _____ Cinderella and the prince dance.

  C. _____ The Shoe lives unhappily ever after.

  D. _____ Cinderella meets her fairy godmother.

  E. _____ Girls all over the kingdom try on the Shoe.

  F. _____ The Shoe realizes that Cinderella has dirty feet.

5. This question has two parts.

First, answer Part A. Then, answer Part B.

Part A

In paragraph 5, what is the meaning of the word "ensemble"?

A. band

B. outfit

C. family

D. dance

Part B

Which detail from the story provides a clue to the meaning of "ensemble"?

E. "With her magic wand"

F. "At first, it was exciting"

G. "I looked good with that dress."

H. "transformed Cinderella's rags"

6. What happens after the prince finds the shoe? Use details from the story to support your answer.

_____

_____

_____

The Talking Eggs

A Creole Folktale

1   One day, Blanche was very upset. Her mother was making Blanche walk alone all day out to the old well. Meanwhile her sister Rose got to relax and loll about.

2   When Blanche got there, she saw an old woman. The woman said she would give Blanche food and a bed. Blanche only had to promise not to laugh at anything she saw.

3   After dinner, the old woman twisted off her own head and set it on her knee. She picked bugs from her hair, and when she was done, she popped her head back on. Blanche swallowed a giggle.

4   The next morning before she was to return home, the old woman spoke.

5   "Because you are good, I will give you a present," she said. "Go to the chicken house. Take all of the eggs that tell you to take them. Do not take the eggs that say, 'Do not take me.' On the road back, break these eggs behind you."

6   Again, Blanche did as she was told. Sparkly jewels, shiny gold, and beautiful dresses came out of the broken eggs.

7   She brought home these fine things. Her jealous mother sent Rose into the woods. "You must have fine dresses too," she said.

8   Rose met the old woman. But she laughed at everything she saw.

9   Still, the old woman sent her to the chicken house. Rose ignored her instructions. She took the eggs that said, "Don't take me."

10   As she broke the eggs, snakes and frogs leapt from them. They chased her as she ran and shrieked. When she arrived home, her mother was angry. She sent Rose away to live in the woods.

Name_____ Date_____

To identify the central message of a story, think about what an author is trying to tell you. Ask yourself what moral or lesson the author is expressing in the story.

Home-School Connection

Help your child identify the central message of a story. Read a fable together, like "The Tortoise and the Hare." After reading, ask your child what he or she learned about life or how to act by reading the story. Point out that a story's central message is what the reader and the characters learn.

SAMPLE QUESTION

Why lesson did Rose probably learn in the story? Use details from the story in your answer.

SAMPLE STUDENT ANSWER

Rose probably learned that she should respect what older people tell her to do. The story says she "ignored" the old woman's instructions and ended up being sent "away to live in the woods."

ANSWER: This sentence identifies what Rose probably learned.

DETAIL: This detail supports the answer.

Now refer to "The Talking Eggs" to answer the questions.

1. What is the lesson of "The Talking Eggs"? Use details from the story to support your answer.

_____

_____

_____

2. The old woman says Blanche is "good." How is Blanche good?

    A. She shares her dresses and jewels with her sister.

    B. She does not laugh at what she sees.

    C. She relaxes and lolls about.

    D. She cares for the chickens.

3. Look at the cause-and-effect box.

Cause	Effect
Blanche returns home with her gifts.	

Which of the following statements goes in the "effect" box?

    A. Rose meets the old woman.

    B. Blanche obeys the old woman.

    C. Her mother becomes jealous on behalf of Rose.

    D. Rose is sent away to live in the woods.

4. Read the following events from "The Talking Eggs." Put the events in the correct order on the time line below.

    A. Blanche cracks the eggs.

    B. The old woman twists off her own head.

    C. The old woman sets her head on her knee.

    D. The old woman picks the bugs from her hair.

    E. The old woman sends Rose to the chicken house.

    F. The old woman tells Blanche not to laugh at anything.

1. ____ 2. ____ 3. _____ 4. _____ 5. ____ 6. ____

Name_____ Date_____

5. This question has two parts.

First answer Part A. Then answer Part B.

Part A

In paragraph 9, what is the meaning of the word "instructions"?

A. documents

B. homework

C. orders

D. statements

Part B

Which detail **best** supports your answer to Part A?

E. "She brought home these fine things."

F. "But she laughed at everything she saw."

G. "Still, the old woman sent her to the chicken house."

H. "Sparkly jewels, shiny gold, and beautiful dresses…"

6. Describe how Blanche and Rose's mother treats them differently. Use details from the story to support your answer.

_____

_____

_____

Little Tío

1   From my front door, I see my favorite green ball outside. It's as lonely as me.

2   "Little Tío," says Mama. "Go outside, make new friends. School is starting soon."

3   But I go sit by the TV.

4   Outside in our new neighborhood, there's just a bunch of houses with the doors all closed up. I never see any kids. In the city, everyone would be out on the streets, always ready to play. The older kids taught me soccer. And I taught it to the younger kids. That's how I got the nickname "Little Tío."

5   Every day after school, we'd play ball and then go buy a shaved ice from Benny. I'd have a lime one every time.

6   The day before I left, Edgar and Manny said, "Little Tío, let's go see the *piragüero*. Our treat."

7   We walked to the corner. A bunch of the kids were looking at me. Something was up.

8   "Hey, it's the little uncle. Do you want the usual?" asked Benny.

9   "Sí!" I said. Benny reached into his shaved ice cart. He pulled out a green ball—for me! The kids all laughed. "We're going to miss you!" they said, crowding around.

10 I think now: *I miss you too*.

11 Back at the window, the ball is still not doing what it should—playing. *Just like me*, I think. I push the door open.

12 My sadness melts away once I get kicking. In almost no time, a door opens across the way. It's a kid! I send the green ball soaring—right over the street. And he returns it!

REVIEW THE SKILL

To describe characters in a story, think about their traits and feelings. To better understand characters, look at what they do and what they say.

Home-School Connection

Help your child describe characters. Work together to list the characteristics of your child's favorite movie or book character. Ask your child to focus on what makes this character unique. Ask your child, "What does the character say? How does the character act? What does this show about the character?"

SAMPLE QUESTION

How does Little Tío feel at the beginning of the story? Use details from the story in your answer.

SAMPLE STUDENT ANSWER

Tío feels sad and lonely at the beginning of the story. In the first paragraph, Tío talks about his green ball and says, "It's as lonely as me." That means Tío is lonely.

DESCRIPTION: This sentence describes the character Little Tío and tells how he feels.

DETAIL: The detail "It's as lonely as me" reveals Little Tío's emotions at the beginning of the story. This detail from the text supports the answer.

Now refer to "Little Tío" to answer the following questions.

1. Describe how Little Tío got his nickname. Use details from the story to support your answer.

_____

_____

_____

2. This question has two parts.

First answer Part A. Then answer Part B.

Part A

Which flavor of shaved ice does Little Tío like the most?

A. cherry

B. coconut

C. grape

D. lime

Part B

Which detail from the passage **best** supports your answer in Part A?

E. "I'd have a lime one every time."

F. "Do you want the usual?"

G. "my favorite green ball"

H. "go buy a shaved ice"

3. In paragraph 12, what is the meaning of the word "soaring"?

A. flying

B. kicking

C. skipping

D. humming

4. Look at the cause-and-effect box.

Cause	Effect
	Little Tío goes outside.

Which details from the passage go in the "cause" box?
Choose **two.**

A. Little Tío's mother tells him to make new friends.

B. Little Tío moves to a new neighborhood.

C. Little Tío thinks he should be playing.

D. Little Tío sits by the TV.

E. Little Tío gets hungry.

5. How does Little Tío feel at the end of the story? Use details from the text to support your response.

_____

_____

_____

How Anansi Got Long, Thin Legs

A retelling of a West African myth

1   There once was a spider named Anansi. He had eight short legs and loved to eat—most especially other animals' food.

2   One day Anansi visited his friend Rabbit. Rabbit was cooking greens on her stove.

3   "Stay and have some when they're finished," said Rabbit.

4   Anansi did not want to wait. He had an idea.

5   "I'll spin a web," Anansi said to Rabbit. "I'll tie one end around my leg. You hold the other end. When the greens are finished, pull on the web. Then I'll come eat with you!"

6   Anansi then visited his friend, Monkey. Monkey was cooking beans in his pot.

7   "Mmm," said Anansi. "I just love beans."

8   Monkey invited Anansi to wait until the beans were cooked, but Anansi was impatient. He spun another web. He tied one end to a different leg and gave the other end to Monkey. "Pull this when the beans are ready," he said to Monkey.

9   Anansi visited eight friends that day. He soon had eight webs tied to his legs.

10 "What a great idea," said the greedy spider, quite pleased.

11 As Anansi walked toward the river, he felt a tug. "Rabbit's greens must be ready," he said. But then came another tug—and another! All eight of his legs were pulled at once! His legs began to stretch and stretch.

12 Anansi quickly rolled himself into the river, and the webs washed away.

13 And that is how Anansi the spider got eight long, thin legs— and why he got nothing to eat that day!

REVIEW THE SKILL

The term "plot" means what happens in a story. Often the way a character acts causes events to happen in a plot.

SAMPLE QUESTION

Anansi loved to eat other animals' food. How did this affect the plot? Use details to support your answer.

SAMPLE STUDENT ANSWER

Anansi loved to eat other animals' food. Because of this, Anansi visited a lot of friends who were cooking. He did not stay and eat at one friend's house. Instead, he made plans to eat all of his friends' food.

DETAIL 1: These words show how Anansi's love of other animals' food affected his actions.

DETAIL 2: This sentence explains how it affected the story's plot.

Now refer to the story to answer the following questions.

1. Why does Anansi tell Rabbit he'll spin a web and tie one end to his leg? Use details from the text to support your answer.

_____

_____

_____

2. What is Monkey cooking in his pot?

   A. beans

   B. eggs

   C. hamburgers

   D. soup

3. Look at the cause-and-effect box.

Cause	Effect
	Anansi has eight webs tied to his legs.

Which details from the passage go in the "cause" box? Choose **two.**

   A. Anansi wants to know when his friends are done cooking.

   B. Anansi ties one web to his legs for each of his friends.

   C. Anansi rolls into the river.

   D. Anansi is forgetful.

   E. Anansi is a spider.

4. Read this paragraph from the text again.

> "As Anansi walked toward the river, he felt a tug. 'Rabbit's greens must be ready,' he said. But then came another tug—and another! All eight of his legs were pulled at once! They began to stretch and stretch."

What is the meaning of "tug" in this paragraph?

   A. boat

   B. pull

   C. rub

   D. tie

Conquer New Standards: Literary Text • Grade 3 • © Newmark Learning, LLC

Name_____ Date_____

5. This question has two parts.

First, answer Part A. Then, answer Part B.

Part A

What happens **right after** all of Anansi's legs are pulled at once?

A. Anansi walks toward the river.

B. Anansi's legs get long and thin.

C. Anansi's webs are washed away.

D. Anansi visits eight friends.

Part B

Which detail **best** supports your answer to Part A?

E. "Anansi quickly rolled himself into the river, and the webs washed away."

F. "'What a great idea,' said the greedy spider, quite pleased."

G. "As Anansi walked toward the river, he felt a tug."

H. "His legs began to stretch and stretch."

6. What is the moral of Anansi's story?

_____

_____

_____

Octavia and the Numbers

1   My name is Octavia. Numbers are the things I like best in the world. Can you guess absolutely my most favorite number? It's eight!

2   In Greek, *oct* means "eight." An octopus has eight legs. And I, Octavia, am named for the number eight. That is because I was born on the eighth day of the eighth month, August 8! I also love other numbers too.

3   Ten is a great number. Soraya, my best friend, lives next door at number 10. She makes my days 10 times better than they were before.

4   Another number I love is 25. Our garden produced 25 big purple eggplants this year. Mama made delicious eggplant dip, eggplant stew, and roasted eggplant.

5   The number 65 also means a lot to me. My *pappoùs* retired when he was 65 years old, and he moved in with us. I help him weed and water our garden, and he tells me stories about being a boy in Greece. Sometimes, it's the same story over and over, but that's fine all the same.

6   Infinity is another great number! It means "endless." Stars are infinite. Soraya and I try to count stars from her backyard, but there are so many we always lose track or fall asleep.

7   But maybe my real favorite number is one. It's the number of beginnings. First time meeting my best friend. First time a plant pushes up through the soil. How *pappoùs's* one story always reminds me of why I love him. How Mama cooks my one favorite vegetable heaps of ways. And one of these days, I just might count until forever—starting with one twinkly star.

Name_____ Date_____

To determine the meaning of unfamiliar words, look at nearby words and phrases (called context clues) that suggest what the unfamiliar word might mean.

Home-School Connections

Help your child understand unfamiliar words. Select a handful of fun yet challenging words from a dictionary. Have your child vote for a "word of the day." Post the word in a noticeable place. Make sure to include it in conversation. Quiz your child on its meaning at the end of the day.

SAMPLE QUESTION

What is the origin of the name "Octavia"? Use details from the text to support your answer.

SAMPLE STUDENT ANSWER

The number eight is the source of the name "Octavia." The narrator says that oct means "eight" in Greek. That's why octopus starts with oct. An octopus has eight legs.

DETAIL 1: This detail tells the meaning of the prefix *oct-*.

DETAIL 2: An octopus has eight legs. "Octopus" also starts with *oct-*.

Now refer to the story to answer the following questions.

1. What is another word that has a similar meaning to "absolutely" as it is used in paragraph 1? Use details from the text to support your answer.

_____

_____

_____

2. Which of the following are **synonyms** of the word "produced" as it is used in paragraph 4? Choose **two.**

   A. baked

   B. fed

   C. grew

   D. hatched

   E. made

3. This question has two parts.

   First, answer Part A. Then, answer Part B.

Part A

   Which vegetable does Octavia really enjoy?

   A. carrots

   B. cucumbers

   C. eggplant

   D. squash

Part B

   Which sentences from the passage **best** support your answer in Part A? Choose **two.**

   E. "I also love other numbers too."

   F. "I help him weed and water our garden."

   G. "First time a plant pushes up through the soil."

   H. "How Mama cooks my one favorite vegetable heaps of ways."

   I. "Mama made delicious eggplant dip, eggplant stew, and roasted eggplant."

4. Read the sentence below.

"My *pappoùs* retired when he was 65 years old, and he moved in with us."

Which of the following is **most likely** the meaning of "retired"?

A. *Pappoùs* got a new hobby.

B. *Pappoùs* took a vacation.

C. *Pappoùs* gave up his job.

D. *Pappoùs* got a new job.

5. In paragraph 6, what is the meaning of the phrase "stars are infinite"?

A. Stars are hard to predict and hard to understand.

B. There are more stars than Octavia can count.

C. Stars are the smallest things in the universe.

D. There are a certain number of stars.

6. What does Octavia think of the number one? Use details from the text to support your answer.

_____

_____

_____

Gray Makes a Move

1   Gray the cat had lived in a narrow alley between a firehouse and a restaurant all of his life. The alley was his home.

2   He loved the exciting sound of the fire truck. He loved when the firehouse door opened. Firefighters galloped onto the trucks, and the trucks screamed down the road. He loved the smell of food from the restaurant, and he especially loved the extra food the restaurant owner, Sam, put out for Gray to eat.

3   The alley may have been small. It may have been muddy and damp. But to Gray it was his own majestic castle. His dinners may have been leftover noodles, day-old burgers, and fries. But to Gray it was a meal fit for a prince.

4   *Could there be anything better?* wondered Gray. But not a single thing came to mind.

5   One night, he woke to a *crackle* and a *pop!* A cloud of smoke was swallowing up Sam's restaurant.

6   Gray ran into the firehouse, and he jumped on the chest of the sleeping fire chief. The chief woke and rang the fire bell. The crew jumped into their boots. In the nick of time, they saved Sam's restaurant.

7   "You're a hero!" cried Sam.

8   "We could use a cat like you around," said the fire chief. "Could you help us?"

9   Gray didn't have to think. He knew the answer in his bones. He tiptoed over to the chief and rubbed against her ankle.

10 Gray found a better place to sleep. It was snug and warm next to a firefighter's boot. And Sam still brought him noodles.

REVIEW THE SKILL

The literal meaning of a word is its dictionary definition. But some words have nonliteral meanings. They mean something different than the dictionary definition. Authors use words and phrases with nonliteral meanings to add interest to their story.

Home-School Connections

Help your child understand that nonliteral language is used for effect. Write a list of funny idioms together—for example, "pain in the neck," "a sight for sore eyes," "in a nutshell," and "I've got a bone to pick with you." Discuss what those nonliteral phrases mean and have your child illustrate the list.

SAMPLE QUESTION

What does the word "alley" mean in paragraph 1? Use details from the text to support your answer.

SAMPLE STUDENT ANSWER

An "alley" is a passage between buildings. I know this because the author says Gray lives in a "narrow" place "between a firehouse and a restaurant."

CLUE 1: This statement describes what an alley is.

CLUE 2: This statement gives details from the passage to support the answer.

Now refer to the story to answer the following questions.

1. What does the author mean by saying that firefighters "galloped" onto the trucks? Use details from the text to support your answer.

_____

_____

_____

2. This question has two parts.

First, answer Part A. Then answer Part B.

Part A

What does the word "castle" suggest in paragraph 3?

A. Gray was a king.

B. Gray appreciated his home.

C. Gray liked living next to stone walls.

D. Gray hoped to become very rich some day.

Part B

Which detail from the story **best** supports your answer in Part A?

E. Gray can't think of anywhere better than where he lives now.

F. Gray would rather live in a castle than a firehouse.

G. Gray likes to eat leftover noodles.

H. The alley was muddy and damp.

3. Which of the following is an example of nonliteral language?

A. "It was snug and warm next to a firefighter's boot."

B. "The chief woke and rang the fire bell."

C. "It may have been muddy and damp."

D. "He knew the answer in his bones."

4. Read this sentence from the passage.

"In the nick of time, they saved Sam's restaurant."

What is another way to say "in the nick of"?

A. hold off on

B. on the dot

C. sliced up

D. just in

5. Look at the cause-and-effect box.

Cause	Effect
Gray saves the restaurant.	

Which sentence or phrase from the passage **best** fits in the "effect" box? Choose **two.**

A. "Gray found a better place to sleep."

B. "He loved the exciting sound of the fire truck."

C. "One night, he woke to a *crackle* and a *pop!*"

D. "he jumped on the chest of the sleeping fire chief"

E. "'We could use a cat like you around,' said the fire chief."

6. What is suggested by the sentence "A cloud of smoke was swallowing up Sam's restaurant?" Use details from the text to support your answer.

_____

_____

_____

Excerpt from
Little White Lily

George Macdonald

Little white Lily
Sat by a stone,
Drooping and waiting
Till the sun shone.
5   Little white Lily
Sunshine has fed;
Little white Lily
Is lifting her head.

Little white Lily
10 Drooping with pain,
Waiting and waiting
For the wet rain.
Little white Lily
Holdeth her cup;
15 Rain is fast falling
And filling it up.

Little white Lily
Said: "Good again,
When I am thirsty
20 To have the nice rain.
Now I am stronger,
Now I am cool;
Heat cannot burn me,
My veins are so full."

REVIEW THE SKILL

Texts have different parts. A novel may have chapters, and a story has paragraphs. Poems have lines and groups of lines, called stanzas.

Home-School Connections

Help your child understand the different parts of texts. Go to a library together or gather some books at home. Ask your child to identify a book that contains chapters (such as a novel), then a text that contains paragraphs (such as a newspaper article), and lastly a text that contains stanzas (a poem).

SAMPLE QUESTION

What is being described in the first two lines of the poem? Use details from the poem in your answer.

SAMPLE STUDENT ANSWER

The first two lines describe the lily, using it as a girl's name, and where it is sitting. It is a "little white" flower. Then the author says Lily "sat by a stone."

DETAIL 1: This detail shows how the first two lines describe the lily as a white flower.

DETAIL 2: This detail shows how the first two lines describe where the lily is.

Now refer to the poem to answer the following questions.

1. What does Lily experience in the first stanza of the poem? Use details from the poem in your answer.

_____

_____

_____

Name_____ Date_____

2. How many stanzas are in the excerpt of "Little White Lily"?

   A. 2

   B. 3

   C. 5

   D. 8

3. Reread these lines from the text:

    "Little white Lily

    Drooping with pain,

    Waiting and waiting

    For the wet rain."

How is Lily feeling? Choose **two** answers.

   A. colorful

   B. hurt

   C. lonely

   D. thirsty

   E. tired

4. Where does Lily say that she is stronger after it rains?

   A. the second stanza

   B. the first stanza

   C. the last stanza

   D. the title

Conquer New Standards: Literary Text • Grade 3 • © Newmark Learning, LLC

5. How many lines are in each stanza of the poem?

    A. 2

    B. 4

    C. 6

    D. 8

6. Describe how Lily changes from the beginning of the poem to the end. Use details from the text to support your answer.

_____

_____

_____

The New Menu

1   Most kids hate the food served at school. But the cafeteria at my school is amazing. Kids don't bring their lunches. We wait in long lines to buy our lunches from Mrs. Cook, the school chef.

2   Every Monday, the halls smell of Mrs. Cook's delicious rigatoni. On Tuesdays, our principal, Mr. Lewis, cuts the line in order to get a bowl of Mrs. Cook's homemade chicken noodle soup. On Wednesday, we can't wait for her tender beef and dumplings. Each day of the week is divine.

3   After school, I stop to talk to Mrs. Cook.

4   "Hey, Mrs. Cook, can't wait for your homemade potato pancakes tomorrow!" I say.

5   "Actually, I'll be taking my first vacation in 20 years! My cousin Pierre is filling in."

6   The next day, there's a strange smell in the air—obviously, Pierre is here.

7   "What's he cooking?" Penny asks.

8   "What are we going to do?" cries JJ.

9   No one buys lunch that day. Or the next. People start bringing their lunches, even Mr. Lewis. On Friday, there's a postcard from Mrs. Cook displayed on the cafeteria wall.

10   "To all my friends," she wrote. "I hope you're surviving. It's wonderful to try new things!"

11   Over at the window, Pierre catches my eye and asks, "Won't you try my *pistou* soup?"

12   I think about Mrs. Cook and decide to take a chance. I walk over and take a spoonful. I wave for Penny and JJ to follow. Whatever *pistou* is, it's actually good.

13   The next week, we are so happy that Mrs. Cook is back. And on Fridays, Pierre's *pistou* joins the rotation too.

Conquer New Standards: Literary Text • Grade 3 • © Newmark Learning, LLC

Name_____ Date_____

REVIEW THE SKILL

Authors think about how best to build their stories. Stories tend to introduce characters in the beginning, develop problems in the middle, and show the solutions at the end.

 Home-School Connection

Help your child understand how one event in the story leads to the next. Read the ending of your child's favorite story aloud to your child. Discuss together how the character got to this ending.

SAMPLE QUESTION

How does the first paragraph introduce the idea that the school chef is a good cook? Use details from the story in your answer.

SAMPLE STUDENT ANSWER

The first paragraph lets us know that Mrs. Cook is a good cook. The paragraph says that the "cafeteria at my school is amazing." It also says kids don't bring their lunches. They wait in lines to buy school lunches because Mrs. Cook's food is so good.

CLUE 1: This detail describes the food Mrs. Cook makes at school.

CLUE 2: These details show just how much people like Mrs. Cook's food

Now refer to "The New Menu" to answer the questions.

1. How does the "strange smell in the air" affect the middle of the story? Use details from the story to support your answer.

_____

_____

_____

2. What is the main problem in the story? Use details from the story to support your answer.

_____

_____

_____

3. Paragraph 9 states "No one buys lunch that day." Why does no one buy lunch that day?

   A. because Mrs. Cook did not make her potato pancakes

   B. because Mrs. Cook's cousin is filling in

   C. because Mr. Lewis always cuts in line

   D. because everyone is on vacation

4. Why does the narrator taste Pierre's soup in paragraph 12? Choose **two** answers.

   A. because Pierre asks the narrator to try it

   B. because the narrator forgot to bring a lunch

   C. because the cafeteria at the school is "amazing"

   D. because Penny and JJ say the soup tastes good

   E. because Mrs. Cook wrote that "It's wonderful to try new things"

5. Which detail from the passage **best** supports the idea that Pierre is a good cook?

    A. "Hey, Mrs. Cook, can't wait for your homemade potato pancakes tomorrow!"

    B. "The next week, we are so happy that Mrs. Cook is back."

    C. "And on Fridays, Pierre's *pistou* joins the rotation too."

    D. "I walk over and take a spoonful."

6. This question has two parts.

First, answer Part A. Then, answer Part B.

Part A

Reread this section of the text.

> "No one buys lunch that day. Or the next. People start bringing their lunches, even Mr. Lewis. On Friday, there's a postcard from Mrs. Cook displayed on the cafeteria wall."

What is the meaning of the word "displayed"?

    A. when something is written down

    B. when something is sent in the mail

    C. when something is shared with others

    D. when something is hung where people can see it

Part B

Which detail from the text **best** reveals the meaning of "displayed"?

    E. "on the cafeteria wall"

    F. "there's a postcard"

    G. "to all my friends"

    H. "she wrote"

Walking With Ruby

1   "Who is that?" I ask in a whisper.

2   "Mary, that's Ruby Bridges," says Mama. I look back at the street. Little Ruby has big tall men on each side of her. It's my first day of school, too, but I've only got my mother walking beside me.

3   "What's all the fuss about?" I ask. People are shouting loudly in front of our school, and some people are holding signs. My stomach feels funny.

4   "It's a sad day," Mama says, sighing, "when a little girl can't go to school without so many grown-ups acting so mean and hateful."

5   Mama goes on to explain, "We read about it in the papers, do you remember? Schools in this country have been separated for far too long. The federal courts decided that schools couldn't be separated by a person's skin color and that children of all backgrounds should be able to attend the same school together."

6   Mama kisses my hand and says proudly, "That young girl is the first African American girl to be going to your school. She's quite amazing, huh? Now we just have to help the rest of the world change and treat people right."

7   I look again at Ruby. She is walking tall despite all the commotion. How does she do that? I wonder.

8   "I would like to meet that Ruby Bridges," I say to Mama.

9   Mama gives me a hug. "You will. You sure will."

Name_____ Date_____

REVIEW THE SKILL

Point of view is an opinion, belief, or perspective on something. Identifying a character's points of view can help you better understand a story.

Home-School Connection

Help your child understand that all people and characters have their own point of view. Have your child describe an event you both experienced (such as eating breakfast or going to a sports game). Then you can describe it from your point of view. Together, compare your accounts.

SAMPLE QUESTION

Who is telling the story? Use details from the story to support your answer.

SAMPLE STUDENT ANSWER

A girl named Mary is telling the story.

We know this because she uses the word "I."

In paragraph 2, her mother calls her Mary.

DETAIL 1: The word "I" is used in the story to show that the speaker is Mary, who is a character in the story.

DETAIL 2: The narrator's mother addresses her as "Mary."

Now refer to the story to answer the following questions.

1. How does Mary feel about what's happening on the street? Use details from the story to support your answer.

_____

_____

_____

2. This question has two parts.

First, answer Part A. Then, answer Part B.

Part A

How does Mary's mother feel about Ruby?

A. She is impressed with Ruby.

B. She is disappointed in Ruby.

C. She is confused by Ruby.

D. She is upset with Ruby.

Part B

Which detail from the story **best** supports your answer to Part A?

E. "'I would like to meet that Ruby Bridges,' I say to Mama."

F. "We read about it in the papers, do you remember?"

G. "Little Ruby has big tall men on each side of her."

H. "She's quite amazing, huh?"

3. What is the meaning of the word "commotion" in paragraph 7?

A. people walking somewhere together

B. children acting mean at school

C. people acting noisy and upset

D. a group activity outside

4. What is **most likely** Ruby's point of view in the story? Use details from the story to support your answer.

_____

_____

_____

5. What does Mary notice about Ruby? Choose **two** answers.

    A. that she sighs

    B. that she walks proudly

    C. that she is holding a sign

    D. that Ruby is looking at her

    E. that she is walking with tall men

6. What is Mama's point of view in paragraphs 4 and 5? Use details from the story to support your answer.

_____

_____

_____

Race Day

1 The first day of every month is race day for the birds that live in the rafters of the county airport. Each sparrow, pigeon, robin, and jay get together to race a giant plane. It's the best day of the month for everyone, except me.

2 I'm Len, a housefly. As a fly that likes adventure, I'd love to join race day. "No, you're too slow and you're too small," the birds always say.

3 Here's my view: every one of us would love to be a plane. Just think about how a plane's roar can split the sky. How fast planes can go, zooming people over oceans, mountains, and deserts. How small we ALL are in comparison.

4 I'm determined to be a part of this race day. So I start buzzing in a few ears.

5 "This is the month for flies," I say.

6 "We've told you, Len, this race is for birds only," says Chip the sparrow. "You'll just be too slow."

7 "But don't I have wings too? Don't I have the heart to do it? Isn't that what matters?"

8 A bunch of birds huddle for a moment and then all turn back to face me.

9 "Okay, you're in," says Rocky the pigeon.

10 "You birds are the best!" I say.

11 Moments later, I'm lined up on a runway sign with the rest of the flock. Madge the jay whistles and yells: "READY, SET, GO!"

12 ROAR. The plane tears into the sky. SWOOOOP go the birds right after it. BUZZZzzzzzzzz—I'm right behind!

13 Do I get anywhere near the birds? No! Did anyone come close to beating that plane? Of course not! But on race day, we all have the time of our lives.

Conquer New Standards: Literary Text • Grade 3 • © Newmark Learning, LLC

REVIEW THE SKILL

The narrator is the speaker telling the story. You can determine the narrator's point of view, or perspective, by taking note of what the narrator thinks and feels.

Home-School Connection

Help your child understand a narrator's point of view. If possible, photocopy a page from a few of your child's favorite stories or books. Then ask your child to use a marker to circle words that show the narrator's opinions, thoughts, and feelings. Discuss these details together and ask your child to describe the narrator's point of view.

SAMPLE QUESTION

Who is speaking in the beginning of the story? Use details from the story in your answer.

SAMPLE STUDENT ANSWER

Len, the housefly, is speaking in the beginning of the story. He introduces himself at the beginning of the second paragraph by saying, "I'm Len, a housefly." Len is the narrator of the story. He says, "Here's my view."

DETAIL 1: This detail shows that the narrator is also a character in the story.

DETAIL 2: This detail tells us exactly what the narrator thinks.

Now refer to "Race Day" to answer the questions.

1. How does Len feel about race day? Use details from the story to support your answer.

_____

_____

_____

2. Which detail **best** reveals Len's point of view on race day?

   A. "SWOOOOP go the birds right after it."

   B. "Just think about how a plane's roar can split the sky."

   C. "The first day of every month is race day for the birds ..."

   D. "It's the best day of the month for everyone, except me."

3. What is the **main** problem in the story?

   A. The birds do not fly as fast as the plane.

   B. Len is not allowed to race on race day.

   C. Len does not fly as fast as the birds.

   D. Len does not beat the birds.

4. Which of the following details show the birds' point of view about Len? Choose **two.**

   A. "You'll just be too slow."

   B. "'You birds are the best!' I say."

   C. "Don't I have the heart to do it?"

   D. "BUZZZzzzzzzzz—I'm right behind!"

   E. "'We've told you, Len, this race is for birds only,' says Chip the sparrow."

5. This question has two parts.

First, answer Part A. Then, answer Part B.

Part A

Reread this section of the text.

> "A bunch of birds huddle for a moment and then all turn back to face me."

What is the meaning of the word "huddle" as it is used in this sentence?

   A.   to line up for a race

   B.   to talk about someone else

   C.   to spread out over a large area

   D.   to gather close together for a conversation

Part B

Which clue from the text **best** supports your answer in Part A?

   E.   "says Rocky"

   F.   "for a moment"

   G.   "Okay, you're in"

   H.   "then all turn back around"

6. Describe Len's point of view in paragraph 13. Use details from the story to support your answer.

_____

_____

_____

Fire the Goat and Flim the Goose

An excerpt from *Sand Flat Shadows* by Carl Sandburg

1   They woke up. Fire the Goat took his horns out and put them on. "It's morning now," he said.

2   Flim the Goose took his wings out and put them on. "It's another day now," he said.

3   Then they sat looking. Away off where the sun was coming up, inching and pushing up far across the rim curve of the Big Lake of the Booming Rollers, along the whole line of the east sky, there were people and animals, all black or all so gray they were near black.

4   There was a big horse with his mouth open, ears laid back, front legs thrown in two curves like harvest sickles.

5   There was a camel with two humps, moving slow and grand like he had all the time of all the years of all the world ….

6   There was an elephant without any head, with six short legs. There were many cows. There was a man with a club over his shoulder and a woman with a bundle on the back of her neck.

7   And they marched on. They were going nowhere, it seemed. And they were going slow. They had plenty of time. There was nothing else to do. It was fixed for them to do it, long ago it was fixed. And so they were marching.

REVIEW THE SKILL

To identify mood, look at the text for feeling words. Also look at the illustration. The illustrations and the text work together to create an overall mood.

Home-School Connection

Help your child understand how illustrations contribute to the mood of a story. Talk about the various emotions that your child feels when reading a favorite story. Discuss how those feelings are shown through characters' facial expressions and body language, as well as through the colors and textures of the artwork.

SAMPLE QUESTION

Is the mood of the story funny, sad, or strange? Use details from the text and illustration in your answer.

SAMPLE STUDENT ANSWER

The mood of this story is sad and strange. Fire can take off his horns and Flim can take off his wings. That doesn't happen in real life. The text describes "an elephant without any head, with six short legs." All of those things contribute to the story's sad, strange mood.

DETAIL 1: These details from the text show that the main characters are unusual.

DETAIL 2: These details from the illustration help readers understand the strange mood of the story.

Now refer to "Fire the Goat and Flim the Goose" to answer the following questions.

1. At what time of day does this story take place? How does that affect the mood? Use details from the story and illustration to support your answer.

_____

_____

_____

2. Which of the following **best** describes how Flim is feeling, based on the illustration?

    A. Flim is happy and smiling at his friend Fire.

    B. Flim is concerned and pointing at the sun.

    C. Flim is scared and trying to fly away.

    D. Flim is tired and stretching his wing.

3. This has question two parts.

    First answer Part A. Then answer Part B.

Part A

The story describes a line of people and animals marching. What is the mood of the marching?

A. excited

B. hopeless

C. joyful

D. rageful

Part B

Which detail from the text **best** supports your answer in Part A?

E. "And they marched on."

F. "They had plenty of time."

G. "along the whole line of the east sky"

H. "They were going nowhere, it seemed."

Conquer New Standards: Literary Text • Grade 3 • © Newmark Learning, LLC

4. What is the meaning of "bundle" as it is used in paragraph 6?

    A. a group of things tied together into a sack

    B. to put warm clothes on

    C. a bunch of money

    D. a hairstyle

5. Which details **best** reveal the mood of the story? Pick **two** choices.

    A. "They woke up."

    B. "slow and grand"

    C. "the sun was coming up"

    D. "There was nothing else to do."

    E. "all so gray they were near black"

    F. "the Big Lake of the Booming Rollers"

6. How does the illustration contribute to the mood of the story? Use details from the text and the illustration to support your answer.

_____

_____

_____

Excerpt from
Pittypat and Tippytoe

Eugene Field

All day long they come and go—
Pittypat and Tippytoe;
Footprints up and down the hall,
Playthings scattered on the floor,
5 Finger-marks along the wall,
Tell-tale smudges on the door—
By these presents you shall know
Pittypat and Tippytoe.

Sometimes there are griefs to soothe,
10 Sometimes ruffled brows to smooth;
For (I much regret to say)
Tippytoe and Pittypat
Sometimes interrupt their play
With an internecine spat;
15 Fie, for shame! to quarrel so—
Pittypat and Tippytoe!

And when day is at an end,
There are little duds to mend;
Little frocks are strangely torn,
20 Little shoes great holes reveal,
Little hose, but one day worn,
Rudely yawn at toe and heel!
Who but you could work such woe,
Pittypat and Tippytoe?

Name_____ Date_____

REVIEW THE SKILL

To better understand the characters in a text, look at the accompanying illustrations. Illustrations can show what the characters think, feel, or do.

Home-School Connection

Help your child understand how to deepen his or her understanding of characters by looking at illustrations. Ask your child to draw a favorite TV or book character. Then describe the character aloud based on the picture. Encourage your child to change the drawing or add to the drawing to develop the character.

SAMPLE QUESTION

Who are the people shown in the illustration? Use details from the text and the picture in your answer.

SAMPLE STUDENT ANSWER

The illustration shows Pittypat and Tippytoe, the two characters from the poem. I know this because of the poem's title, "Pittypat and Tippytoe." Stanza 1 says they play "all day," so that makes me think that they are children. The illustration confirms my ideas.

DETAIL 1: The poem's title shows the names of the two characters.

DETAIL 2: The illustration shows two children, which goes along with the description in the text.

Now refer to the excerpt from "Pittypat and Tippytoe" to answer the following questions.

1. Describe how the characters look. Use details from the text and the illustration to support your answer.

   _____

   _____

2. Which line from the poem describes the characters' clothes as shown in the illustration?

   A. "Sometimes there are griefs to soothe"

   B. "Tell-tale smudges on the door"

   C. "Sometimes interrupt their play"

   D. "There are little duds to mend"

3. Look at the illustration. What are Pittypat and Tippytoe feeling?

   A. happy

   B. hungry

   C. sad

   D. sleepy

4. What are synonyms for the word "quarrel" in line 15? Pick **two** choices.

   A. argue

   B. disobey

   C. fight

   D. spit

   E. tattle

5. This question has two parts.

First, answer Part A. Then, answer Part B.

Part A

What is **most likely** on the wall in the illustration?

A. artwork

B. fingerprints

C. footprints

D. presents

Part B

Which line from the text supports your answer in Part A?

E. "All day long they come and go"

F. "By these presents you shall know"

G. "Finger-marks along the wall"

H. "Sometimes ruffled brows to smooth"

6. Describe what Pittypat and Tippytoe do to the room they are in. Use details from the text and the illustration to support your answer.

_____

_____

_____

A Mysterious Matter

1 When my family came down to breakfast this morning, there were papers scattered all over. But before we had gone to bed, there were three neat piles on the kitchen table. One was my stack of homework, the second was my brother's art project, and the third was Mom's work files.

2 We all looked at our old dog. He was snoring in his doggie bed. But there was no way Scooter could have gotten on the table. He was too short and, well, too lazy.

3 Mom pointed to the still ceiling fan and asked, "Did someone turn that on and off?" But no one had used the fan.

4 All day, the mystery bothered me. In school, my teacher noticed I was wrinkling my brow.

5 "Brandon, is something wrong?" my teacher asked.

6 "I'm stumped about something," I said, scratching my head.

7 "Think about what Arthur Conan Doyle wrote: 'The world is full of obvious things which nobody by any chance ever observes,'" she said.

8 Later, I looked around the kitchen. Scooter was sleeping as usual. He flopped over and the fan turned on! Then he flopped over the other way and the fan turned back off.

9 I nudged Scooter out of his bed. Underneath was the cause of all the mischief. Scooter HAD done it!

REVIEW THE SKILL

Illustrations can help you understand a story's setting. Look at the pictures for details. The pictures might tell you when or where events are happening.

Home-School Connection

Help your child practice identifying how an illustration can show setting. Find a new picture book. Ask your child to close his or her eyes as you read the book aloud. Ask your child to describe the setting. Then show the illustrations. Ask, "How do the illustrations change your understanding of where the story takes place?"

SAMPLE QUESTION

Where does most of this story take place? Use details from the text to support your answer.

SAMPLE STUDENT ANSWER

Mostly, this story takes place in a kitchen.
The story describes a "kitchen table" and coming down for "breakfast."

DETAIL 1: Details in the illustration show the setting of the story.

DETAIL 2: The first line of text also indicates where the story takes place.

Now refer to "A Mysterious Matter" and the illustration to answer the following questions.

1. What do you know about the kitchen? Use details from the text and illustration to support your answer.

_____

_____

_____

2. Where did the papers start before they ended up on the floor?

   A. Scooter's bed

   B. Mom's briefcase

   C. the kitchen table

   D. Brandon's backpack

3. Where is the dog in the story?

   A. in the sink

   B. on the table

   C. in the dog's dish

   D. in his doggie bed

4. How did the ceiling fan turn on in paragraph 8? Use details from the text and the illustration to support your answer.

   _____

   _____

   _____

5. This question has two parts.

First, answer Part A. Then, answer Part B.

Part A

What is the meaning of the word "stumped" in paragraph 6?

A. confused about something

B. sitting on part of a tree

C. crawling on one's knees

D. working hard at something

Part B

Which details from the story **best** reveal the meaning of the word "stumped"? Choose **two**.

E. "He was too short and, well, too lazy."

F. "scratching my head"

G. "wrinkling my brow"

H. "I nudged Scooter"

I. "I looked around"

6. What does Brandon feel at the end of the story? Use details from the text and the illustration to support your answer.

_____

_____

_____

Zula Speaks

Danielle Martin

1   "Mama, why is today's event called a photo scavenger hunt?" Hector asked from the back seat.

2   Mama caught Hector's glance in her rearview mirror. "We take pictures so we don't damage nature, Hector," she explained. "By taking pictures, we collect items without touching them."

3   There were about twenty people waiting for Ranger Tandy at the community park. Hector, his friend Marcus, his mother, and their dog Zula would be Team Orange. Ranger Tandy distributed a checklist for the scavenger hunt. At 1 p.m., all six teams scattered down the main trail to search the park for the items.

4   Immediately Marcus noticed mushrooms growing on a tree. Then Hector found a patch of wild berry bushes. Mama followed a birdsong to snap a photo of a cardinal on a fence.

5   Team Orange searched for an hour. They had photos of all the items on the list but one: a squirrel. Mama suggested that the woods were too full of people. The squirrels were afraid to move around.

6   Just then, Hector noticed Zula pulling her leash toward a tree. She sniffed the trunk and looked high into the branches. This gave Hector an idea.

7   "Let's all hide behind that bush for a few minutes," Hector whispered. "Have the camera ready, Mama."

8   Team Orange hid for about ten minutes. Then, two squirrels cautiously climbed down the trunk of a tree—Zula's tree! Mama snapped the photo and looked at Hector with pride.

9   "How did you know the squirrels would be in that tree, Hector?" Marcus asked.

10 "Zula told me," Hector said with a smile.

Sadie Signs

Danielle Martin

1   "Look again at the board, Sadie," Frank, her teacher, said in sign language.

2   Sadie the gorilla saw the symbol on the board. She saw the pictures near it: apple, ant, and acorn. But she did not understand what the symbol had to do with the pictures.

3   "We'll try again tomorrow, Sadie," Frank said. "You worked hard today," he signed. "Thank you."

4   Sadie shook Frank's hand as he left like she did every day. Then Sadie's keeper Andrew came in. Sadie was happy to see Andrew because he was carrying her dinner. Andrew set down the basket of fruits and vegetables, and Sadie gave Andrew his daily hug.

5   Sadie enjoyed this time of day. She liked her fresh, delicious food. She also liked Andrew. Sadie began eating some lettuce, and Andrew started sweeping the floor in Sadie's room.

6   Andrew pointed to the board and signed to Sadie, "Frank" and "letter *A.*" He looked over at Sadie's face.

7   Sadie signed "Yes" and "I don't understand."

8   Andrew smiled and signed "sounds." Then out loud he said, "It's all about sounds, Sadie." He walked to the board and pointed to the letter *A.*

9   "This letter makes the sound that begins these words: apple, ant, acorn, alligator," he explained, emphasizing the beginning sound of each word. "Another example is my name." Then he pointed to his name "Andrew" sewn into his uniform shirt. Then he pointed back to the *A* on the board.

10 Suddenly, Sadie understood! The symbol on the board shows what sound to make in the people language. She was excited to meet with her teacher Frank tomorrow!

REVIEW THE SKILL

You can compare and contrast the themes in two stories by considering how their big ideas or messages are similar or different.

Home-School Connection

Help your child practice comparing the themes of different stories. Select two books or movies that have similar themes, like helping others or wanting to be someone else. Have your child tell you the plot of one of the stories, making notes in the left column of a T-chart. Then discuss the other story. Say, "[Story A] has a main character who [desire, action, etc.]. What does the main character in [Story B] want/ do? Is that the same or different than in [Story A]?" Continue prompting your child to make comparisons between the two stories' ideas.

SAMPLE QUESTION

The titles of the passages give a clue to the theme of each story. Describe how they are similar and how they are different.

SAMPLE STUDENT ANSWER

Both titles have to do with communication.

The first passage is "Zula Speaks."

Speaking is a way of communicating.

The second passage is "Sadie Signs."

Sign language is a form of communicating, too.

CLUE 1: The title of the first passage shows that its theme must be about communicating.

CLUE 2: The title of the second passage shows that its theme is about communicating, too.

Now refer to both stories to answer the questions.

1. Compare and contrast how Hector and his mom communicate to how Sadie and Andrew communicate. Use details from the stories to support your answer.

_____

_____

_____

2. What things does Sadie enjoy? Pick **two** choices.

    A. She likes visits from Andrew.

    B. She likes hunting squirrels.

    C. She likes fresh vegetables.

    D. She likes taking pictures.

    E. She likes math lessons.

3. Identify several of the ways the characters communicate with each other in "Sadie Signs" and "Zula Speaks." Use details from each story to support your answer.

    _____

    _____

    _____

4. What sound does Hector's mom hear in the park?

    A. a birdsong

    B. a whistle

    C. a shout

    D. a bark

5. This question has two parts.

First, answer Part A. Then, answer Part B.

Part A

How are Hector and Andrew **alike**?

A. They both teach animals.

B. They both feed animals food.

C. They both use sign language.

D. They both watch animals closely.

Part B

Which details **best** support your answer in Part A? Choose **two.**

E. "He looked over at Sadie's face."

F. "Then Hector found a patch of wild berry bushes."

G. "Andrew set down the basket of fruits and vegetables …"

H. "Just then, Hector noticed Zula pulling her leash toward a tree."

I. "Mama followed a birdsong to snap a photo of a cardinal on a fence."

6. How are the themes in "Zula Speaks" and "Sadie Signs" similar and different? Use details from both stories to support your answer.

_____

_____

_____

Conquer New Standards: Literary Text • Grade 3 • © Newmark Learning, LLC

7. Read the following sentences from "Zula Speaks."

"How did you know the squirrels would be in that tree, Hector?" Marcus asked.

"Zula told me," Hector said with a smile.

Which message is **best** supported by these sentences?

A. Living things can communicate only by speaking the same language.

B. Animals and humans can communicate and understand each other.

C. Dogs act in certain ways that everyone can understand.

D. Loving an animal helps you understand it better.

8. Read the sentence from "Zula Speaks."

"Ranger Tandy distributed a checklist for the scavenger hunt. At 1 p.m., all six teams scattered down the main trail to search the park for the items."

Which words are **synonyms** for "distributed"? Pick **two** choices.

A. kept for oneself

B. requested back

C. gave to others

D. hid from sight

E. handed out

Excerpt from
"The Old Lobsterman"

John Townsend Trowbridge

Just back from a beach of sand and shells,
   And shingle the tides leave oozy and dank,
Summer and winter the old man dwells
   In his low brown house on the river bank.
5 Tempest and sea-fog sweep the hoar
And wrinkled sand-drifts round his door,
Where often I see him sit, as gray
And weather-beaten and lonely as they.

Coarse grasses wave on the arid swells
10   In the wind; and two dwarf poplar-trees
Seem hung all over with silver bells
   That tinkle and twinkle in sun and breeze.
All else is desolate sand and stone:
And here the old lobsterman lives alone:
15 Nor other companionship has he
But to sit in his house and gaze at the sea.

Excerpt from
"Menotomy Lake (Spy Pond)"

John Townsend Trowbridge

Down through the dark evergreens slants the mild light:

    I know every cove, every moist indentation,

Where mosses and violets ever invite

    To some still unexperienced, fresh exploration.

5   The mud-turtle, sunning his shield on a log,

    Slides off with a splash as my paddle approaches;

Beside the green island I silence the frog,

    In warm, sunny shallows I startle the roaches.

I glide under branches where rank above rank

10   From the lake grow the trees, bending over its bosom;

Or lie in my boat on some flower-starred bank,

    And drink in delight from each bird-song and blossom.

Above me the robins are building their nest;

    The finches are here,—singing throats by the dozen;

15 The catbird, complaining, or mocking the rest;

    The wing-spotted blackbird, sweet bobolink's cousin ….

Springtime and Maytime,—revive in my heart

    All the springs of my youth, with their sweetness and splendor:

O years, that so softly take wing and depart!

20   O perfume! O memories pensive and tender!

Compare/Contrast Settings of Two Texts

REVIEW THE SKILL

Setting is where or when the events in a story happen. You can compare and contrast two texts by looking at how their settings are similar and different.

Home-School Connection

Help your child compare and contrast settings. Ask your child to write a description of a favorite outdoor place, including details like plants, animals, colors, and descriptions of weather. Then prompt your child to think about how the setting changes when the seasons change. For example, if your child described the favorite place in the summer, have him or her think about how it changes in the winter.

SAMPLE QUESTION

What are the settings of the two poems? Use details from each poem to support your answer.

SAMPLE STUDENT ANSWER

The first poem takes place at the beach. The first line says, "a beach of sand and shells."

DETAIL 1: In the first poem, the setting is stated in the first line.

The second poem takes place at a lake. Its title, "Menotomy Lake (Spy Pond)," tells me the setting.

DETAIL 2: The title of the second poem states its setting.

Now refer to the poems to answer the following questions.

1. Compare and contrast the seasons in the poems. Use details from both poems in your answer.

_____

_____

_____

2. What details about setting are in **both** poems? Pick **two** choices.

    A. flowers

    B. sand

    C. stones

    D. sun

    E. water

3. Which statement **best** describes the difference in the weather in the two poems?

    A. The first describes stormy, wet weather. The second describes mild, dry weather.

    B. The first describes a hurricane. The second describes a good day for swimming.

    C. The first describes dry weather. The second describes a rainy day.

    D. The first describes a hot day. The second describes a cold day.

4. Which of the following statements **best** describes the structure of the poems?

    A. Both poems are made up of stanzas containing four lines.

    B. Both poems are made up of stanzas containing eight lines.

    C. Both poems have a third person narrator.

    D. Both poems contain lines that rhyme.

5. This question has two parts.

First, answer Part A. Then, answer Part B.

Part A

Reread these lines from "The Old Lobsterman."

> "Coarse grasses wave on the arid swells
>
>   In the wind; and two dwarf poplar-trees
>
> Seem hung all over with silver bells
>
>   That tinkle and twinkle in sun and breeze."

What is the meaning of "wave" as it is used in these lines?

A. to move back and forth in the wind

B. the choppy part of the ocean

C. to gesture with a hand

D. to grow straight

Part B

Which statement **best** supports your answer in Part A?

E. Grass along the seashore is straight and stiff.

F. The swells of wind would make the grass move back and forth.

G. Grass growing below the ocean's surface floats on waves to shore.

H. Sometimes grass takes on human qualities, like being able to wave.

6. What theme is expressed by **both** poems? Use details from both poems to support your answer.

_____

_____

_____

7. Reread these lines of "The Old Lobsterman."

"Nor other companionship has he

But to sit in his house and gaze at the sea."

What is the meaning of the word "gaze" as it is used in these lines?

A. goes swimming

B. listens to

C. looks at

D. talks to

8. Compare and contrast how the settings contribute to the mood of each poem. Use details from both poems to support your answer.

_____

_____

_____

Adapted excerpt from
"Honor Bright, President"

Sarah Cory Rippey

1   When Honor Bright went to live in the country the very first thing he asked for was real live geese to join the farm.

2   "Will you feed them every day?" asked his father.

3   "Yes, papa," said the little boy. When he promised, he always kept his word.

4   "Quack, quack!" cried Mr. and Mrs. Goose the day Honor Bright's father brought them home. What a fine place!

5   Honor Bright was as good as his word, and the geese grew fatter, and fatter, and fatter.

6   "Good morning, Mr. T. Cat" cried Mr. and Mrs. Goose early one morning. "Had your breakfast?"

7   "Of course," answered Mr. T. Cat. "Honor Bright always feeds me the very first thing."

8   "You must be mistaken!" cried Mr. and Mrs. Goose. "Honor Bright always feeds us first."

9   "But Honor Bright gives my children their breakfast very early!" cackled Mother Hen.

10 "Well," squeaked Father Rabbit Gray, "we've all had breakfast, and that's the main thing. Now, let's make Honor Bright president, because he's so good."

11 Just then Honor Bright came out. "Hail, President Honor Bright!" they all cried.

12 Honor Bright thought they said, "I love you" and really, it meant the same thing.

Adapted excerpt from
"The Going-To Club"

Sarah Cory Rippey

1   The Going-To Club had only one member. Bobby Brant was that member. It was his mother who named him the Going-To Club. It always took at least two askings to get Bobby to do anything. Bobby was always "going to."

2   One spring Bobby had a very fine new kite that he and his father had made together. But something was wrong. Instead of sailing up gracefully, the Skylark pitched about so violently that Bobby had to wind it in.

3   Just then he heard Mary Jane calling, "Bobby, will you get me some water?"

4   "All right," cried Bobby.

5   "Bob-by-y!"

6   "I'm going to," answered the Going-To Club impatiently, and straightway forgot all about it.

7   "Mary Jane," said Bobby, "will you help me fix my kite?"

8   A twinkle came into Mary Jane's eyes. "All right, Bobby," she said, and went on to the well.

9   "Will you?" urged Bobby, as she came back with her pail full.

10 "I'm going to."

11 Bobby followed Mary Jane.

12 "Mary Jane—"

13 "I'm going to," she promised.

14 Mary Jane dried her hands and picked up the kite.

15 "Tail's too long," she said. "And, by the way, Bobby," she added, "what do you think about the Going-To Club now?"

16 Bobby grinned and hung his head.

Name_____ Date_____

"Plot" refers to the events that happen in a story. To compare and contrast two stories, look at the events in the beginning, middle, and end of both stories.

Home-School Connection

Help your child compare the plots of different stories. Select two stories. Ask your child to read the beginning of both stories. Then discuss the details and events in both beginnings. Ask your child to identify how they are alike or different. Do the same for the middles and ends of both stories.

SAMPLE QUESTION

Read the first paragraph of each story. Compare and contrast how the author begins each story.

SAMPLE STUDENT ANSWER

Both stories begin by introducing a boy: Honor Bright and Bobby Brant. In "Honor Bright, President," the author introduces a boy who moves to the country. In "The Going-To Club," we don't know where Bobby Brant lives.

DETAIL 1: These details are similarities between the two stories.

DETAIL 2: These details show differences between the two stories.

Now refer to both stories to answer the questions.

1. Describe what Honor and Bobby are doing at the beginning of the stories. Use details from each story to support your answer.

    _____

    _____

    _____

2. What is **similar** about the beginnings of both stories?

   A. The beginnings show the main characters in a difficult situation.

   B. The beginnings tell how the characters solve their problems.

   C. The beginnings describe where the main character lives.

   D. The beginnings give details about the main characters.

3. How are the middle sections of each story **similar**?

   A. The middle sections show what happens when the main characters do not keep their promise.

   B. The middle sections show how other characters feel and act toward the main characters.

   C. The middle sections show how the main characters feel when facing challenges.

   D. The middle sections show how the main characters solve serious problems.

4. What is the meaning of the word "urged" in paragraph 9 of "The Going-To Club"?

   A. invited

   B. led

   C. pressured

   D. waited

Name_____ Date_____

5. This question has two parts.

First, answer Part A. Then, answer Part B.

Part A

In "The Going-To Club," why does Mary Jane say "I'm going to" to Bobby?

A. to make him realize how she feels when he says "I'm going to"

B. to show that she promises to help him right away

C. to try to make him stop asking her for help

D. to convince him to help her get water

Part B

Which details from the passage **best** support your answer in Part A? Choose **two.**

E. "Bobby followed Mary Jane."

F. "Just then he heard Mary Jane calling."

G. "A twinkle came into Mary Jane's eyes."

H. "she added, 'what do you think about the Going-To Club now?'"

I. "Going-To Club had only one member. Bobby Brant was that member."

6. Describe the differences between the ends of both stories. Use details from each story to support your answer.

_____

_____

_____

7. Compare and contrast the overall plots of both stories. Use details from both stories to support your answer.

_____

_____

_____

8. This question has two parts.

First, answer Part A. Then, answer Part B.

Part A

How are Honor Bright and Bobby Brant different?

A. Honor Bright has to be asked several times to do things, whereas Bobby Brant does things without being asked.

B. Honor Bright does things without being asked, whereas Bobby Brant has to be asked several times to do things.

C. Honor Bright learns how to treat the farm animals nicely, whereas Bobby Brant does not learn how to treat others nicely.

D. Honor Bright does not make the farm animals happy, whereas Bobby Brant makes Mary Jane very happy.

Part B

Which of the following **best** supports your answer in Part A?

E. Honor Bright "always kept his word," and Bobby Brant "always took at least two askings."

F. Honor Bright wanted "live geese," and Bobby Brant wanted to help Mary Jane get "some water."

G. Honor Bright did not feed the geese "first," and Bobby Brant "grinned" at Mary Jane.

H. The farm animals promise to help Honor Bright, whereas Mary Jane wants to make Bobby Brant "president."

Unit 1: Discussion Prompts

1. The detail that helped me understand the text the most was …

2. Using the details in the text helped because …

3. I think this skill is important because …

 AT-HOME ACTIVITIES: *Details Race*

Stand with your child against the wall on the side of a room. Take turns recalling a detail from the text in the passage. Check that the detail is remembered correctly. Each time a person correctly recalls a detail, the person can take one step forward. The person who correctly recalls the most details and gets to the other side of the room first wins!

Unit 2: Discussion Prompts

1. I am still curious about …

2. I am confused and have questions about …

3. Answering my questions with details helped me by …

 AT-HOME ACTIVITIES: *Question-and-Answer Shopping Spree*

Get sticky notes and canned food. Together with your child, brainstorm questions about the text in the unit. Write one question on each sticky note and place the note on a can of food. Tell your child he or she has one minute to try to answer as many questions on the cans as possible. Set the timer and let the shopping spree begin! Take turns until all the cans are used.

Unit 3: Discussion Prompts

1. The story was mostly about …

2. What I remember most about the story is …

3. Recounting the story helps me because …

 AT-HOME ACTIVITIES: *Story Stone*

Instruct your child to paint the words "Story Stone" on a stone. Then, if possible, gather together three or more people for this activity. Sit with your child (sit in a circle if you have enough people). Hand the stone to your child and ask him or her to tell a brief story. Then, ask your child to hand the story to the next person (or back to you). The person with the stone recounts the most important details of the story. This person then hands the stone to the next person, who tells another story. Keep passing the stone, telling stories, and recounting their most important details.

Unit 4: Discussion Prompts

1. This story showed how people should …

2. The characters in the story learned that …

3. Identifying the central message, lesson, or moral helped me …

 AT-HOME ACTIVITIES: *Good Behavior Poster*

Use a large piece of paper or poster board. Ask your child to tell you what morals, lessons, or central messages he or she has learned from books and movies. Pick five and list them along the top of the paper. Then encourage him or her to draw a picture under each moral, lesson, or message that tells about it. For example, your child might say, "I learned that I should feel thankful about who I am when I watched the movie *The Little Mermaid*. Ariel almost lost her voice to be human." You can write "Feel thankful for who I am," and your child can draw a picture of Ariel.

Unit 5: Discussion Prompts

1. When ... happened in the story, this character ...

2. The character who is the most ... was ...

3. Describing characters helped me by ...

 AT-HOME ACTIVITIES: *Improv!*

Take turns acting out an improvised scene with your child. Either you or your child should volunteer to act first. The person who is not acting should suggest two things: (1) a situation or event and (2) a characteristic or feeling. The person acting should pretend to have that characteristic or feeling and act out the situation or event. Discuss with your child how having a certain characteristic or feeling influenced his or her response to the situation or event.

Unit 6: Discussion Prompts

1. When the character did ..., it made ... happen.

2. ... character often responds by ...

3. ... character was important to the story because ...

 AT-HOME ACTIVITIES: *Domino Effect*

Discuss the unit text or another story your child enjoys. Ask your child to tell you how the main character's actions cause the story to happen. Encourage your child to tell you how this happens step-by-step in the story. Write down the steps your child tells you. Then work with your child to line up dominos or bricks to represent each step. Push the first domino and watch the "story unfold" as all the other dominos fall. Discuss how the main character's actions contributed to the plot.

Unit 7: Discussion Prompts

1. I can use context clues to …

2. When I read and find a confusing word, I can …

3. Figuring out the meaning of words helped me …

 AT-HOME ACTIVITIES: *Guess My Sketch*

Read over the unit text with your child, circling the words your child does not know or finds confusing. Say one of the words aloud, and then read the paragraph in which the word occurs. Next, draw a picture of what the word means. Ask your child to guess the meaning of the word. Keep drawing clues until your child guesses correctly. Then go back to the story and read the sentence in which the word occurs, discussing how the meaning of the word helps your child better understand the story. Continue taking turns doing this for all the circled words.

Conquer New Standards: Literary Text • Grade 3 • © Newmark Learning, LLC

Unit 8: Discussion Prompts

1. An example of a literal word is …

2. An example of a nonliteral word is …

3. The skill in this unit helped me …

 AT-HOME ACTIVITIES: *Quirky Language*

Create a book with your child. Fold several sheets of paper in half, and then staple along the fold. Open the book, and write an example of nonliteral language on the left page; this can be a colloquialism or common saying. Ask your child what the phrase means, and encourage your child to draw a picture of this on the right page. Work together to complete the book.

Unit 9: Discussion Prompts

1. A chapter is …

2. A stanza is …

3. A scene is …

 AT-HOME ACTIVITIES: *Library Treasure Hunt*

Come up with a list of parts of texts you and your child could find in a treasure hunt. This list should include one example of a chapter, stanza, and scene. Then, go together to a library and compete to complete the treasure hunt. Whoever finds all the items on the list first wins!

Unit 10: Discussion Prompts

1. The events in this story …
2. The story in the unit ended by …
3. Thinking about how texts build helped me …

 AT-HOME ACTIVITIES: *Tell a Tale*

Ask your child to identify his or her favorite fairy tale, story, or legend. Tell your child to write a brief version of this story in which the events in the story are told in the order in which they happened. Then, work with your child to tell the story in different ways. For example, you and your child could tell the story going in reverse, or back in time, starting with the most recent event. Or you and your child could tell the tale as a series of memories, in which the main character has an action in the present and then a memory. Or you and your child could tell the tale using a structure of cause-and-effect in which each part of the story is about how a character caused an event to happen.

Unit 11: Discussion Prompts

1. The character ... thinks/feels ...

2. A character who thinks/feels differently is ...

3. This skill helped me understand the text by ...

 AT-HOME ACTIVITIES: *Try On a New Point of View*

Make masks with your child. You can use construction paper, paper bags with holes cut out for eyes, and markers. Instruct your child to make a different mask to represent each character in the unit's text. Then, with your child, try on the masks and act out that character's part of the story. Ask your child how it felt to pretend to be that character. Ask your child if he or she has insights into that character's thoughts, feelings, and opinions.

Conquer New Standards: Literary Text • Grade 3 • © Newmark Learning, LLC

Unit 12: Discussion Prompts

1. One type of narrator is …

2. Narrators use words like …

3. Identifying the narrator helped me …

 AT-HOME ACTIVITIES: *Be the Narrator*

Help your child better understand the role of a narrator in a book. Pick an activity your child enjoys, such as playing at the park. Take your child to the park. Before your child plays, ask your child to tell a story about the other children playing. Explain to your child that this is like a narrator who is outside of the story and uses the words "she," "he," or "they." Your child might say, "Those kids are racing on the monkey bars. I see the child who is working hard, and now just won!" Then encourage your child to play. When your child is done, ask your child to tell the story again. Explain to your child that this is like a narrator who is a character in the story and uses the word "I." Your child might say, "I was racing with the other kids on the monkey bars. I had tried very hard to win and got second place."

Unit 13: Discussion Prompts

1. I got a sense of … mood from this picture …

2. Overall, the picture made me feel …

3. Looking at the picture helped me …

 AT-HOME ACTIVITIES: *Moody Paintings*

Discuss different moods with your child, such as happy, scary, anxious, and loving. Then encourage your child to paint a picture to reflect each mood. You can brainstorm ideas for each painting together. For example, your child might say that a picture of flower expresses a happy mood. Then, you could ask your child how to paint the picture to portray the mood of happiness as much as possible, such as making sure the setting and the color of the flower portray happiness.

     Conquer New Standards: Literary Text • Grade 3 • © Newmark Learning, LLC

Unit 14: Discussion Prompts

1. The illustrations showed me that the characters …

2. I figured out that … would happen next based on the illustration …

3. Using details in the illustration helped me …

 AT-HOME ACTIVITIES: *Let's Look at the Pictures*

Pick out a picture book (from your home, the library, or while visiting a bookstore). Look over all the pictures with your child, but cover up the words with your hands. After looking at all the pictures, ask your child about who the characters are and how they act. Then read the book. Talk about what you and your child learned about the characters from just looking at the pictures and what you and your child learned from reading the book.

Unit 15: Discussion Prompts

1. The first illustration showed me the setting …

2. I could see how the setting changed in the illustration …

3. Using details in illustrations helped me …

 AT-HOME ACTIVITIES: *I Spy*

Read a book with illustrations with your child. Stop on a page with illustrations that show some aspect of the setting. Then play "I Spy" with your child. Identify something you see in the setting and describe it to your child, saying "I spy with my little eye…." Your child has to identify what you are describing in the illustration of the setting. You and your child can take turns doing this, pointing out more and more details in the illustration of the setting.

Conquer New Standards: Literary Text • Grade 3 • © Newmark Learning, LLC

Unit 16: Discussion Prompts

1. The themes of the texts were alike in these ways …

2. The themes of the texts were different in these ways …

3. Thinking about ways the themes were alike and different helped me …

 AT-HOME ACTIVITIES: *Story Hopscotch*

Using chalk, draw a hopscotch play area on a sidewalk or play surface. Number the squares 1 through 10. Use one color for five of the squares, and a different color for the remaining five squares. Explain to your child that landing on one color means he or she should identify a theme that is shared by the two texts, and landing on the other color means he or she should identify themes that were different in the two texts. Instruct your child to throw a small pebble or paper ball onto the hopscotch play area. Then, tell your child to hop on one foot to whatever square the pebble fell onto. Then he or she should tell about the two texts depending on the square's color. Take turns playing hopscotch together.

Unit 17: Discussion Prompts

1. The settings of the texts were alike in these ways ...

2. The settings of the texts were different in these ways ...

3. Thinking about ways the settings were alike and different helped me ...

 AT-HOME ACTIVITIES: *Spot the Differences*

Ask your child to pick a setting described in a story he or she enjoys. Encourage your child to draw this setting, and then to draw it a second time with up to five changes. Then, look at your child's pair of drawings and work to spot the five differences. Then you can create two drawings depicting a setting with up to five changes and encourage your child to view your pair of drawings and spot the five differences.

Unit 18: Discussion Prompts

1. The plots of the texts were alike in these ways ...

2. The plots of the texts were different in these ways ...

3. Thinking about ways the plots were alike and different helped me ...

 AT-HOME ACTIVITIES: *Pick Your Path Board Game*

Use a large piece of construction paper or cardboard and markers. Instruct your child to draw a circle and write "Start" inside of it. Then ask your child how his or her story should start. Encourage your child to draw a box near the "Start" circle and write or draw the beginning of the story. Explain to your child that he or she is drawing the "path" of the story. Next, encourage your child to draw a "fork" in the path. At this fork, your child can imagine two different ways the story could develop and write these as two options. Continue working with your child to develop this board game. When your child has filled up the board, you and your child can play using game pieces from other household games.

Answer Key

Unit 1

pages 14–17

1. Sample answer: In the beginning of the poem, Freddy won't speak. When Maisie tries to get him to speak, he acts "bored." But by the end of the poem, Freddy starts speaking. He speaks "endlessly, throughout every whole long day." So he goes from silent and bored to talkative and excited.

2. Sample answer: I think Maisie goes out to play when Freddy is talking because she doesn't want to hear him talk anymore. I think this because the stanza says Freddy talked "all through the day." He talked "endlessly," repeating the same words over and over.

3. **Part A   D**   In line 6, the word "retreat" is used to describe how Freddy moves.

   Part B   H   The poem says he moves "to the back of his cage," so "move backward" is the meaning of "retreat."

4. **A, C, E**   The words "twitter," "shrieks," and "cheep" all describe different sounds a bird might make.

5. (1) **A** Maisie gets a new parrot.
   (2) **C** Maisie sings songs to Freddy.
   (3) **E** Freddy looks bored and turns away. (4) **D** Maisie buys a mirror for Freddy. (5) **F** Freddy says "Hey, give us a cheep!" (6) **B** Maisie goes outside to play.

6. Sample answer: By the end of the poem, Freddy most likely feels excited. He sees a bird in the mirror and he keeps looking, which shows that he is excited. Also, he finally starts talking and then he keeps talking all the time. So this also shows he probably feels excited.

Conquer New Standards: Literary Text • Grade 3 • © Newmark Learning, LLC

Answer Key

Unit 2

pages 18–21

1. Sample answer: When the author goes to bed, the sky is still blue. There are "birds still hopping on the tree" and "grown-up people's feet/ Still going past me in the street."

2. **A, E**   The author says he can see a bird on the tree. This suggests that the tree is just outside his window.

3. **D** "Candlelight" is a compound word made up of the words "candle" and "light." If you know the meaning of each of those words, you can figure out the meaning of "candlelight."

4. **B** The first two lines of the poem say that, in winter, the author gets up at night and gets dressed.

5. **Part A   D**

   Part A   H   The author wants to do other things besides go to sleep. For example, he "should like so much to play." Going to bed when it is still light outside makes him sad.

6. Sample answer: The author addresses the reader in the first line of the last stanza: "And does it not seem hard to you..." That tells us the author thinks the reader would also find it hard to go to bed when it is still light outside.

Answer Key

Unit 3

pages 22–25

1. Sample answer: The Shoe doesn't really like Cinderella. It says her feet are dirty, and when she dances at the ball, they get sweaty.

2. **B** The Shoe is telling us the story, but Cinderella doesn't meet the Shoe until her fairy godmother gives it to her before the ball.

3. **B** Cinderella's feet get sweaty because she wears them while she "danced and danced."

4. (1) **D** Cinderella meets her fairy godmother. (2) **F** The Shoe realizes that Cinderella has dirty feet. (3) **B** Cinderella and the prince dance. (4) **A** The prince finds the Shoe. (5) **E** Girls all over the kingdom try on the shoe. (6) **C** The Shoe lives unhappily ever after.

5. **Part A   B**   In this story, the word "ensemble" means "outfit."

    Part B   G   The Shoe tells the reader, "I looked good with that dress." The Shoe and the dress together make the ensemble, or outfit.

6. Sample answer: The prince takes the Shoe around the kingdom for all the women to try on. The Shoe is not happy about having to touch even more yucky feet.

Conquer New Standards: Literary Text • Grade 3 • © Newmark Learning, LLC

Answer Key

Unit 4

pages 26–29

1. Sample answer: The lesson of the story is that good behavior is rewarded. Blanche listens to the old woman and gets nice presents. Rose ignores her and gets chased by snakes and frogs.

2. **B** In paragraph 2, the old woman asks Blanche not to laugh, and Blanche stops herself from laughing in paragraph 3. Then in paragraph 5, the old woman says she is "good."

3. **C** After Blanche returns home with her gifts, her mother becomes jealous. She wants Rose to have nice things too.

4. (1) **F** The old woman tells Blanche not to laugh at anything. (2) **B** The old woman twists off her own head. (3) **C** The old woman sets her head on her knee. (4) **D** The old woman picks the bugs from her hair. (5) **A** Blanche cracks the eggs. (6) **E** The old woman sends Rose to the chicken house.

5. **Part A**   **C**   The word "instructions" means "orders."

    Part B   **G**   The story shows how Blanche manages to listen and act respectfully. The old woman orders the girls not to pick eggs that said "Don't take me." These were her instructions, or orders.

6. Sample answer: The mother is mean to Blanche, but she wants nice things for Rose.

Answer Key

Unit 5

pages 30–33

1. Sample answer: Little Tío learned soccer from the older kids. He then taught soccer to the younger kids. He was like a very young uncle to them.

2. **Part A**   **D**   Little Tío's favorite flavor is "lime."

   Part B   **E**   The detail that he gets a lime one "every time" supports the answer to Part A.

3. **A** Little Tío kicks the ball high "over the street." This detail supports answer choice A.

4. **A, C**   Little Tío thinks to himself that he should be playing with the ball. Also, his mother tells him to go outside to play and make friends.

5. Sample answer: When Little Tío starts playing with his ball, his sadness melts away. He feels more excited after kicking the ball over to the kid across the street. I know this because the author uses exclamation points when sharing Little Tío's thoughts.

Answer Key

Unit 6

pages 34–37

1. Sample answer: Anansi doesn't want to wait around for Rabbit to finish cooking, but he still wants some of Rabbit's greens. Anansi will know the greens are ready when Rabbit pulls on the string attached to Anansi's leg.

2. **A** Monkey is cooking beans.

3. **A, B** At each of his eight friends' homes, Anansi ties one web to his legs. This is so he will know when his friends are done cooking.

4. **B** The author says that "All eight of his legs were pulled at once!" That reveals that the meaning of "tug" in this story is "pull."

5. **Part A   B**   After Anansi's legs are all pulled at once (in paragraph 11), they are likely to become long and thin.

   Part B   H   As soon as his legs are pulled, his legs stretch. This causes his legs to become "long" and "thin."

6. Sample answer: The moral of the story is that it is important to be patient. Anansi was not patient and he was greedy. In the end, he "got nothing to eat that day" and his legs were changed.

Answer Key

Unit 7

pages 38–41

1. Sample answer: Eight is the number that Octavia likes "best." "Absolutely" is a strong way to say that it is definitely her favorite. So I think the word "definitely" could also be used.

2. **C, E**   Gardens grow vegetables. You could also say that vegetables are made in a garden. "Produced," therefore, has a similar meaning to the words "grew" or "made."

3. **Part A**   **C**   Octavia loves eggplant.

   Part B   **H, I**   Octavia talks about all the ways her mother cooks eggplant and also refers to eggplant as her favorite: "How Mama cooks my one favorite vegetable heaps of ways."

4. **C** To "retire" must mean to "give up a job" or to stop working. Octavia's grandfather had decided to stop working.

5. **B** "Infinity" means "endless." Octavia and Soraya are not able to count all the stars because there are so many stars.

6. Sample answer: She thinks the number one might be her real favorite number. To her, it means new beginnings. It helps her remember the first time significant events happened to her.

Answer Key

Unit 8

pages 42–45

1. Sample answer: To "gallop" is to move fast like a horse does. While this does not mean that the firefighters are horses, it does mean that the firefighters move quickly.

2. **Part A**   **B**   Gray thinks of his home as a castle because he really likes where he lives.

   Part B   **E**   When Gray calls the alley his "home," this shows how much he loves it and thinks highly of it.

3. **D** "He knew the answer in his bones" is nonliteral language. Gray does not actually check with his bones to determine the answer. This phrase means that Gray knows the answer very deeply within himself.

4. **D** The sentence shows that the firefighters got there "just in" time because they saved the restaurant.

5. **A, E**   Gray saves the restaurant and the fire chief invites Gray to move in. Sleeping in the firehouse is better than sleeping in the alley.

6. Sample answer: The sentence does not literally mean that the smoke was eating the restaurant. It means that there was so much smoke that it was covering the restaurant so it was as if the smoke was swallowing it up.

Answer Key

Unit 9

pages 46–49

1. Sample answer: In the first stanza, Lily is droopy because she needs the sun to come out. Then the sun comes out, and Lily lifts her head.

2. **B** The excerpt shows three groups of lines, which means there are three stanzas.

3. **B, D** These lines show how Lily is waiting and waiting for rain. This must mean she is thirsty. She is so thirsty that she is "drooping with pain." So she is also hurt.

4. **C** In the last stanza, Lily says "Now I am stronger..."

5. **D** Each stanza contains 8 lines.

6. Sample answer: At the beginning of the poem, Lily doesn't feel good. She needs the sun to come out. The sun comes out and then she feels better. In the following stanzas, Lily needs the rain to come out because she is thirsty. The rain fills her up. Having been fed by both the sun and the rain, Lily feels happy at the end of the poem.

Conquer New Standards: Literary Text • Grade 3 • © Newmark Learning, LLC

Answer Key

Unit 10

pages 50–53

1. Sample answer: The strange "smell in the air" is the smell of Pierre's cooking. As a result, the kids in the school decide not to buy lunch, as they normally would do.

2. Sample answer: The main problem in the story is that Mrs. Cook, the school chef, goes on vacation. That means the kids cannot have her cooking.

3. **B** Mrs. Cook's cousin was filling in as school chef. The students did not think his food would be good, and as a result, no one bought school lunch.

4. **A, E** The narrator remembers Mrs. Cook's note that encourages the kids to try new things. Immediately after that, Pierre invites the narrator to try the soup.

5. **C** After trying the *pistou,* the narrator finds out that he likes it. Other kids try it too. Even though they are happy that Mrs. Cook comes back, they add Pierre's food to the menu. This detail supports the idea that Pierre's soup really does taste good.

6. **Part A**   **D**   "Displayed" means "when something is hung where people can see it."

   Part B   **E**   The postcard is "on the cafeteria wall." This is where you would hang, or display, Mrs. Cook's postcard.

Answer Key

Unit 11

pages 54–57

1. Sample answer: She is nervous when she sees the crowd in front of the school. She says, "My stomach feels funny."

2. **Part A**   **A**   Mary's mother is impressed because Ruby is the first African American student to be going to Mary's school.

   Part B   **H**   Mary's mother says, "She's quite amazing, huh?" The word "amazing" shows that Mary's mother is impressed.

3. **C** A "commotion" is a noisy activity, usually done by a group of people. We know this because Ruby is walking into school as people shout.

4. Sample answer: The text says that Ruby is "walking tall despite all the commotion." This suggests that Ruby's point of view is that she should have equal rights and be able to go to a school attended by white students. She may agree with Mary's mother that schools should not be segregated, or separated.

5. **B, E**   Mary notices the men walking alongside Ruby and asks her mother about it. Mary also observes her "walking tall," or proudly.

6. Sample answer: Mama says that "Schools in this country have been separated for far too long." Her point of view is that she agrees with the federal courts, who "decided that schools couldn't be separated by a person's skin color." She is also sad that some grown-ups are acting mean and thinks that they should stop.

Answer Key

Unit 12

pages 58–61

1. Sample answer: Len would really like to join race day with the birds. He says he "likes adventure" and would "love to join race day."

2. **D** Len's point of view is that he loves race day. The detail that "It's the best day of the month" shows this point of view.

3. **B** The main problem in the story is that Len is not allowed to race. Most of the details in the story have to do with this problem and with Len trying to solve this problem.

4. **A, E**   At first, the birds will not let Len race on race day. They say that the race is "for birds only" and that he is "too slow."

5. **Part A   D**   The word "huddle" means to "gather close together for a conversation."

   Part B   H   The detail about how the birds "then all turn back to face me" suggests that they had all been turned facing each other close together, or huddled in conversation.

6. Sample answer: Len's point of view is that racing is fun even if you don't win. He says that the birds did not beat the plane, and he didn't beat the birds. But he thinks that none of this matters because they all have so much fun.

Answer Key

Unit 13

pages 62–65

1. Sample answer: The story takes place early in the morning. The text says "It's morning now," and the illustration shows a sun rising. While normally mornings might have a happy mood, in this story, the morning feels upsetting. The people and animals are "all so gray" that they are nearby black against the sunlight. So this seems gloomy.

2. **B** The picture shows Flim, the goose, pointing his wing at the sun.

3. **Part A**   **B**   The line of animals and people is hopeless.

   Part B   **H**   The detail "they were going nowhere" supports the idea that the mood is hopelessness.

4. **A** In the passage, "bundle" is a noun that means "a group of things tied together into a sack."

5. **D, E**   The details that there "was nothing else to do" and that everyone was "gray" reveal the mood of sadness or hopelessness in the story.

6. Sample answer: The illustration shows that Flim is pointing. He is pointing at sun and possibly also at the people the text says are marching. The illustration also shows that the sky is dark. These details bring out the sad mood of the story.

Conquer New Standards: Literary Text • Grade 3 • © Newmark Learning, LLC

Answer Key

Unit 14

pages 66–69

1. Sample answer: Pittypat and Tippytoe are little kids. They both have stains on their clothing. One is wearing stripes. The poem also says their clothes are "torn."

2. **D** The illustration shows that both Pittypat and Tippytoe have messy clothing with holes. So the line referring to how their "duds" need to be mended is the correct answer.

3. **C** The illustration shows the characters frowning and crying, so they look sad.

4. **A, C** The poem says that Pittypat and Tippytoe "interrupt their play" to have a "spat." I bet they are fighting, or arguing. "To quarrel" must mean "to fight" or "to argue."

5. **Part A   B   ** The illustration makes the marks look hand-shaped, which supports answer choice B.

   **Part B   G   ** The poem describes "finger-marks along the wall," so the marks on the wall are probably fingerprints.

6. Sample answer: Pittypat and Tippytoe scatter their toys all over the floor. They leave "finger-marks along the wall" and "tell-tale smudges on the door." The illustration shows that they make a mess.

Answer Key

Unit 15

pages 70–73

1. Sample answer: The kitchen is where the characters eat breakfast. There is a ceiling fan, and there is also a dog bed for Scooter, the family's dog.

2. **C** The narrator says that there were "three neat piles on the kitchen table" before the family had gone to bed the night before.

3. **D** Paragraph 2 states "He was snoring in his doggie bed."

4. Sample answer: Paragraph 8 says the dog "flopped over and the fan turned on!" Then the dog "flopped over the other way and the fan turned back off." The illustration shows that the ceiling fan remote control is in the doggie bed, so I inferred that the dog turned the fan on and off by rolling onto the remote control.

5. **Part A**   **A**   The word "stumped" means "confused."

   Part B   **F, G**   Brandon's actions of "wrinkling" his brow and "scratching" his head reveal his confusion.

6. Sample answer: The story suggests that Brandon is excited. While the story doesn't describe Brandon, it does include exclamation points to show his excitement ("the fan turned on!" and "done it!"). The illustration shows Brandon smiling.

Conquer New Standards: Literary Text • Grade 3 • © Newmark Learning, LLC

Answer Key

Unit 16

pages 74–79

1. Sample answer: Hector and his Mom talk to each other. I know that because their words are between quotation marks. The author uses words like "asked," "said," and "explained" to show when they are saying something aloud. Andrew and Sadie the gorilla also communicate. But they use a lot of "sign language."

2. **A, C** Sadie the gorilla enjoys the time of day when Andrew comes to feed her fresh food. She eats lettuce in the story.

3. Sample answer: In "Sadie Signs," the characters communicate by "sign language." Andrew and Frank also speak out loud and write on the board. In "Zula Speaks," the characters mainly communicate by speaking, but Zula the dog also communicates with the way she acts. For example, she pulls toward a tree to show she is interested in the tree.

4. **A** Hector's mom follows the song of a cardinal.

5. **Part A** **D** Both Hector and Andrew watch animals closely. Hector watches Zula, and Andrew watches Sadie the gorilla.

   Part B **E, H** Answer choices E shows Andrew looking closely at Sadie the gorilla, and answer choice H shows Hector closely watching Zula.

6. The themes of "Zula Speaks" and "Sadie Signs" are similar and different. Both stories share a theme about how living things can talk or communicate in many different ways, such as by speaking, writing, or moving. But in "Zula Speaks," the theme is about how paying attention to animals can help you win or succeed, such as how Hector helps his team find a squirrel because he notices when Zula tugs toward a tree. The theme of "Sadie Speaks" is about how learning how to communicate is important and can make living things feel excited and happy.

7. **B** This detail shows how Hector was able to understand Zula, a dog.

8. **C, E** The teams need a checklist so that they know which items they need to find. Ranger Tandy must have handed out the checklists to each team. When she distributed the checklists, she was giving them to others.

Answer Key

Unit 17

pages 80–85

1. Sample answer: The first poem seems to talk about all the seasons, saying "Summer and winter the old man dwells," whereas the second poem is focused on the season of spring ("Springtime and Maytime").

2. **D, E**   Both poems mention the sun. The first poem talks about coarse grasses that "tinkle and twinkle in sun and breeze." The second poem describes "warm, sunny shallows." The poems also talk about bodies of water. In the first poem, the low brown house sits on a river bank. In the second poem, the narrator paddles on a lake.

3. **A** "Tempest and sea-fog" describes the wet, windy weather in the first poem. "In warm, sunny shallows" describes the pleasant, dry weather in the second poem.

4. **D** Both poems are made up of stanzas, but the first poem contains eight-line stanzas and the second poem contains four-line stanzas. Both poems do use rhyme throughout as part of their structure.

5. **Part A   A**   In these lines, the word "wave" means to move due to "swells" of "wind."

    Part B   F   In the poem, the wind would most likely make the grass move back and forth.

6. Sample answer: While the poems are very different, they share a theme of the importance of nature in human life. In the first poem, the old lobsterman doesn't have any "companionship" except for the sea. In the second poem, the narrator remembers "all the springs of my youth." Both poems speak of the power of nature.

7. **C** The old man is in his house. That means he's not swimming. He's not speaking to the sea or listening to it from inside his house, so he must be looking at it.

8. Sample answer: In "The Old Lobsterman" the windy, gray beach contributes to the feeling of loneliness and sadness. In "Menotomy Lake (Spy Pond)," the descriptions of the sunny, warm lake contribute to the happy mood of the poem.

126

Answer Key

Unit 18

pages 86–91

1. Sample answer: Honor Bright is asking for "real live geese" to go along with the other animals at the new farm. Bobby Brant is trying to fly a kite.

2. **D** The beginnings of both stories describe their respective main characters.

3. **B** In the middle of "Honor Bright, President," the animals discuss what they think and feel about Honor Bright. The middle of "The Going-To Club" shows Mary Jane's actions toward Bobby Brant.

4. **C** In this story, Bobby keeps asking Mary Jane to help him. So to "urge" means to pressure or push someone or something.

5. **Part A**   **A**

   Part B   **G, H**   Mary Jane shows Bobby how bad it feels when people say they will help but then forget about it. She even tells him what he tells everyone else: "I'm going to."

6. Sample answer: The ends of the stories are very different. Honor Bright is rewarded at the end. The animals all love him and cheer for him. Bobby Brant is taught a lesson. He learns that it's not fair to tell people you're going to help them when you really just intend to ignore them.

7. Sample answer: The plots of the stories are similar and different. Both stories are about a young boy. But Honor Bright always "kept his word." He promises to feed the geese and he cares for the farm animals, so the animals like him and make him "president." Bobby Brant does not keep his word and has to be asked several times to do something. As a result, Mary Jane does not help him with his kite right away.

8. **Part A**   **B**

   Part B   **E**   The stories state that Honor Bright always "kept his word," whereas Bobby Brant "always took at least two askings."

Notes

_____

_____

_____

_____

_____

_____

_____

_____

_____

_____

_____